The Blueprint

Is God's Bible Design Linear or *Circular*?

The Story of God's Perfect Plan for His Creation

By Earl A. Clampett

Distributed by
Simple Truth Ministries Inc.
San Diego, California, USA

The Blueprint
Copyright 2016 by Earl A. Clampett

Simple Truth Ministries Inc.
P.O. Box 27263
San Diego, CA 92198

Email: rev.earl@simpletruthministries.net

Website: www.simpletruthministries.net

Phone: (858) 432-Earl
3275

Cover Artist Design: Paul Churchward
Layout: Dewayne Williams
Editor: CeCe O'Donnell

ISBN 13:978-1533579041

"Ballad of East and West"
by Rudyard Kipling

Oh' East is East and West is West, and never the twain shall meet,

Till earth and sky stand presently at God's Judgment Seat;

But there is neither East nor West, border, nor breed, nor birth,

when two strong men stand face to face,

though they come from the ends of the earth.

Foreword

Have you ever been out on the open road, oblivious to your surroundings until you spot a highway sign indicating that your earlier route was the exact opposite of your intended destination?

What do most people do once they discover they're headed in the wrong direction? They get off the current path, they turn around and head the opposite way.

It has happened to me. You feel the fool and wish to correct your error in the fastest way possible.

Deception is an enigmatic experience. If someone were to ask us if we're deceived about something, we're often unable to effectively answer the question since the intrinsic nature of a deceptive belief is that it renders us unable to recognize our duped condition. Our being tricked about an issue usually suggests a lack of wariness on our part.

Not being mindful that we're in the midst of spiritual warfare can cost us dearly.

Our struggling against a fallen angelic host requires our attention and watchful eye. We need to be able to detect trickery in order to avoid dangerous snares. Our angelic adversary, Lucifer, along with his fallen hordes, employ clever deceptive tactics such as mixing lies and distorted reality with just enough truth to make us fall. These devices are designed to deter us from our paths of divine destiny.

The stakes are huge. And the consequences are eternal.

In 2005, Christian pollster George Barna sounded a clarion call in his report on the health of the Christian Church in America. He explained that there exists a long-term absence of real change on key religious beliefs and behaviors that scream for an about-face and an earth-shaking approach to spiritual growth.

I concur with Barna. The Church as we know it has lost its salt and light. Our Christian witness has been undermined by our acceptance of destructive distortions of the original Hebrew-based Scriptures. Our enemy has craftily infiltrated God's Hebrew Gospel (the Gospel based on its original Hebrew concepts of time and purpose) with Hellenized philosophies that have resulted in deadly detours for the Church.

Platonic, Gnostic, Western perversions have crept into the divinely inspired original Hebrew Scriptures during the formative years of the Christian Church. In addition, **Western/linear** thinking distorted the **Hebrew circular/cyclical** expressions of the Father's divine goals. These distortions adhered themselves to the early blueprint fabric of the Church, bringing about radical doctrinal confusions. The results? We discredited our Hebrew foundations, resulting in them being downplayed or even ignored entirely.

The Bible does not promote two different religions, nor is it only fifty percent relevant. It contains one Hebrew, singular, revelatory account. It is *our*—both Jew *and* Gentile—Father's blueprint to restore mankind's relationship with Him and reinstall His heavenly government back on our earth (Isaiah 9:6-7; Psalms 2:8-9).

The Father's original blueprint design laid out in the first two chapters of Genesis has never changed and it never will. God finishes that which He begins. No one, not rebellious angels nor rebellious men, has the authority to change His blueprint. The Architect is sovereign.

"For I am the Lord, I do not change" (Malachi 3:6).

Acknowledgements

I would like to acknowledge the profound influence of Dr. Robert B. Thompson in his Kingdom of God teachings, writings, sermons and thoughts. Many of the concepts taught by Dr. Thompson formed my foundation of understanding from which the Lord expanded with additional comprehension and concepts through ministries, education and experiences divinely provided to me.

I am also grateful to my pastor Reverend Wayne Clarke (Capt. U.S.N. Ret.) for his availability and the generous giving of his time in assisting me with the completion of my bible school studies.

My colleague Assistant Pastor Dewayne Williams graciously invested his time coordinating the formatting and layout design of this work.

CeCe O'Donnell spent endless hours editing this book displaying the patience of Job.

Elliott Stearns, a Bible scholar in his own right, selflessly invested hours of review with essential corrections and additions to this text.

Lastly, I am grateful to my wife, Vilma, who for 2.5 years tolerated an often-absentee husband while working on this project.

Introduction

Have you ever wondered if there is a simple and straightforward way to explain the complexities of the Bible?

As a jail chaplain for almost ten years, I found myself in desperate need of a direct and uncomplicated way to explain God's blueprint plan for mankind within a jail setting and classroom environment.

One of the occupational hazards of jail ministry is the total unpredictability of security disruptions along with the limited time available to complete one's teaching. Since security is always a high priority concern in the jail environment, our Sunday evening services with the inmates were often suspended due to lockdowns. The constant interruptions were frustrating to say the least. When the sheriff deputies were forced to cut a service short due to a security issue, there was no negotiating or convincing them for a short extension to complete our teaching, much less to wrap up with a final prayer or an altar call.

Jail ministry is in a constant state of flux. The inmates' situations are highly fluid due to prisoners awaiting everything from initial court arraignment on criminal charges, to a full-blown trial, to sentencing, to awaiting transportation to a state prison. In some ministry situations, I would see an inmate anywhere from on a single occasion to as many as twenty times, depending on his individual circumstance.

Due to all these obstacles, the ultimate challenge as a jail minister was how to present the good news of the Gospel in a brief, impactful and long-lasting way that would be life-changing, even if I only had a single opportunity to teach the Gospel of the Kingdom message.

What I had to do next became clear: *I needed to change my presentation.*

So I went to the Lord in prayer and asked Him to reveal a completely revolutionary manner of explaining the Gospel message. His revelation to me through the Holy Spirit forever changed the way I performed jail ministry. In fact, it was so profound that it also changed how I explained the Gospel to all groups of listeners from that point on, irrespective of the setting.

What I heard from Him was that the entire story of the Bible could be explained with *five* words all beginning with the same letter of the alphabet: "R".

Additionally, the Lord later showed me that the entire Bible message is *circular* and not in a straight line. Initially, I did not understand why the Lord insisted that the five words were to be taught in a circular design. Nevertheless, I began to teach the Bible account in a straightforward, five-word, circular format.

After beginning to teach the newly revealed paradigm to the inmates, the atmosphere within the jail walls began to drastically change. Soon, even the deputies began approaching us, curious to know exactly what we were teaching in those Sunday night sessions. We answered that we were not just sharing the Gospel of Salvation to the inmates, but that we were also now explaining the *Gospel of the Kingdom* and *how* to put it into action.

When we asked the deputies what prompted their inquiries regarding what was being taught inside those jail multipurpose rooms, their response both amazed and encouraged us beyond anything we could have earlier imagined.

The deputies explained that the inmates were no longer behaving like typical prisoners. They were becoming polite not only to their fellow inmates, but also to the guards themselves. The guards reported that they were beginning to hear words like "please", "thank you" and "good morning" from the same individuals who used to spit in their faces and with whom there had been extreme tension and distrust.

Jail gangs began to dissolve, and inmate-organized Bible studies comprised of various ethnic members began to take their place. We watched in disbelief as Caucasian and Black inmates began attending our Spanish-speaking services, which required us to turn the single-language service into a bilingual teaching. All became hungry for the "real deal" and for what actually worked.

The inmates' worlds began to change with the introduction of the Gospel of the Kingdom. Many complained that they had been "saved" in jail multiple times through hearing the Salvation message. However, few had ever really experienced any real transformation in their behavior. No one had ever explained to them **the details** of God's goals intended for mankind through the Christian experience. No one had ever taught them God's present and future Kingdom roles for His people. Additionally, they wanted to experience the actual freedom that comes to the captives and the oppressed when the complete Gospel is preached as expressed by Christ:

The Spirit of the Lord is upon Me, because He has anointed Me to preach the gospel to the poor; He has sent me to heal the brokenhearted, to proclaim liberty to the captives and recovery of sight to the blind, to set at liberty those who are oppressed; to proclaim the acceptable year of the Lord" (Luke 4:18–19).

The Holy Spirit began to show us some hands-on, Kingdom-type experiments that the inmates could immediately implement within their jail setting in order to demonstrate the *power* of the Kingdom of God. Each week, we would check in and conduct follow-up surveys to monitor the progress of these experiments. The results were nothing short of astonishing, and the outcomes caused even the deputies to notice the monumental changes taking place within such an oppressive environment.

We taught the inmates the Father's powerful goal from the well-known Lord's Prayer of *"Thy Kingdom come, Thy will be done"* (Matthew 6:10). God continually answered our prayer by *first* bringing Kingdom **order** followed by demonstrations of His **power** through changing hearts, minds and behaviors. Soon the inmates themselves became the ones through whom God established His Kingdom order and resulting peace—right in the dark pit of their county jail! The love and light of God began to penetrate and transform the stifling atmosphere of those four walls, and many of those inmates would never be the same.

I later realized that based on their universal application, these same experiments that were yielding such phenomenal results within a jail setting could be taught to anybody. The last line of the Lord's Prayer certainly applies here where we see, *"For Yours is the kingdom **and the power** and the glory forever. Amen"* (Matthew 6:13). (Emphasis added.) The tangible outcome of praying this simple phrase is always impressive— and immediate.

Some Christian teachers instruct that we are transitioning from the Church Age to the Kingdom Age. The Gospel of Salvation is certainly the essential **beginning** of the overall Gospel message of good news, but the Gospel of Salvation is the "kickoff" event, *not* the final touchdown score.

The Gospel of the Kingdom explains ***how the circular story ends***. And how the story ends may just surprise you.

The Kingdom of God message includes God's blueprint for mankind and explains how a spiritual invasion of rebellion perverted God's perfect earthly blueprint. The Kingdom message includes the Father's *circular,* restorative answer to the disastrous consequences of rebellion. His perfect answer includes defeating and replacing the rebellious government of Satan.

The Kingdom account can be observed in the books of the Pentateuch, starting with Genesis; the Historical books; the Psalms, Proverbs, and Ecclesiastes; the major and minor prophetical books; the four gospels, especially the Gospel of Matthew; Paul's letters, Peter's letters, the epistles of James, John and Jude; and wrapping up with the book of Revelation— all of which reveal that the Bible account is a *circular* story as opposed to a linear experience.

You are invited to climb the mountain to explore the unfolding vistas of how the majestic plan of God's *circular* blueprint is being revealed so powerfully and wonderfully in these exciting and challenging times.

Fastening your seatbelts is highly recommended.

Table of Contents

Chapter 1

The Entire Bible in Five Words?

I am often asked by listening audiences whether it's really possible to describe the entire Bible story in just five words.

After informing them that not only is it possible, I add that it is actually logical. Perhaps for the first time, it allows the different aspects of Scripture to finally come together and make sense.

It is easy for the reader to remember the five words since each of them begins with the same letter: **"R"**.

In my 2003 publication entitled "God's Got a Problem (On His Hands)", I explained the five **"R's"** that sum up the Bible in the following way:

1. God created man to have a *relationship* with Him.
2. God created man for *rulership* over His works and creation on earth.
3. Man *rebelled* against God. Man fell away from God and died.
4. God then set up a program of *redemption* to rescue man from his fallen state.
5. God will *restore* man to his previous stature.

We will extensively examine each of these five words in later chapters of the book.

Suffice it to say for now, **the first two "R" words—** *relationship and rulership*—deal with the original blueprint of God's goals regarding His creation. This included man's roles within God's perfect blueprint plan.

Then God said, "Let Us make man in Our image, according to Our likeness; let them have **dominion** *over the fish of the sea, over the birds of the air, and over the cattle, over all the earth and over every creeping thing that creeps on the earth."*
So God created man in His own image; in the image of God He created him; male and female He created them.

Then God blessed them, and God said to them, "Be fruitful and multiply; fill the earth and **subdue** *it; have* **dominion** *over the fish of the sea, over the birds of the air, and over every living thing that moves on the earth."*

And God said, "See, I have given you every herb that yields seed which is on the face of all the earth, and every tree whose fruit yields seed, to you it shall be for food. "Also, to every beast of the earth, to every bird of the air, and to every thing that creeps on the earth, in which there is life, I have given every green herb for food"; and it was so. Then God saw everything that He had made, and indeed **it was very good**. *So the evening and the morning were the sixth day* (Genesis 1:26–31). (Emphasis added.)

God sought out a divine-human *relationship* with His creation of man and woman. He was not only man's Creator, He was also mankind's Father. He loved, nurtured and provided for His first children. The intimate relationship of man and God supplied the essence of man's life. The relationship with God *was* life. And it was designed to last forever.

*"And this is **eternal life**, that they may **know You**, the only true God, and Jesus Christ whom You have sent"* (John 17:3). (Emphasis added.)

As a loving father, God desired to assign man the meaningful responsibility of stewarding and shepherding all of His earthly creation. In reality, God wished that mankind would be the **rulers** of the earth, having dominion over the entirety of creation.

*"Then the Lord God took the man and put him in the Garden of Eden **to tend and keep it**. Out of the ground the Lord God formed every beast of the field and every bird of the air, **and brought them to Adam to see what he would call them**. And whatever Adam called each living creature, that was its name"* (Genesis 2:15,19). (Emphasis added.)

The **third *"R"*** deals with spiritual **rebellion** against God. In the midst of bringing his spiritual rebellion to earth, Satan ended up corrupting mankind's divine destiny. He robbed us of our very lives by separating our first parents from God. He robbed us of our inheritance of the earth and its nations. He robbed us of our destiny of earthly rule and stewardship. He achieved his master plan by spreading among all mankind his toxic rebellion of distrust and disobedience against God (Genesis 3).

*"**How you are fallen from heaven**, oh Lucifer, son of the morning! How you are cut down to the ground, you who weakened the nations! For you have said in your heart: I will ascend into heaven, **I will exalt my throne** above the stars of God; I will also sit on the mount of the congregation on the farthest sides of the north; I will ascend above the heights of the clouds, **I will be like the Most High** (Isaiah 14:12–14). (Emphasis added).*

With the successful deception of our first earthly parents in the Garden, we as mankind *lost* our *relationship* with the Father. We became dead men walking. Without relationship with the Father through His Son Jesus, man has *no life*. Our first parents chose rebellion (disobedience) over obedience. They chose death over life.

The soul who sins shall die (Ezekiel 18:4).

As a result of their deadly choice, we in turn *lost* our divinely ordained *identity* and *purpose*. Through our original parents' signing on to Lucifer's rebellion, God's goals and roles for us as His children became distorted. By aligning themselves with Satan's rebellion against God, Adam and Eve squandered His planned destiny for mankind's rulership over the earth. The enemy stole away our heritage. We lost our birthright to property (the earth), our rank (to rule and reign with the Lord) and our privilege (as children of God).

One of the topics we will later explore is whether God ever changed His mind regarding His eternal purpose for man's destiny. We will also study whether ancient, foreign, contrary, non-biblical teachings of heresy (i.e. Platonism, Gnosticism, antinomianism, etc.) have penetrated the Church's understanding of God's original design for mankind.

The *third "R" word, rebellion*, deals with a problem that began in the spiritual realm (Heaven) with a spiritual creature (Lucifer) that *later* came down to earth and poisoned God's creation, including mankind. The problem of rebellion, chaos, confusion and disobedience continues to be more prevalent than ever on earth today.

How God intends to deal once and for all with this continuing problem is the purpose of the *fourth "R" word: redemption*. The idea of redemption explains the brilliance of the Father in outwitting and conquering the rebellion of a fallen angel. Through the ultimate gesture of love, God sent His only begotten Son in *human* form to repurchase mankind by acting as an obedient sacrifice to assuage the Father's anger. As a result, mankind can finally be *reconciled back to the Father* by crossing the Son's obedient "bridge of blood".

*"I am the way the truth and the life. No one comes to the **Father** except through me"* (John 14:6). (Emphasis added.)

*"And they sang a new song, saying: You are worthy to take the scroll, And to open its seals; for **You were slain, And have redeemed us to God by Your blood"** (Revelation 5:9–10). (Emphasis added.)

As we cross that "bridge of blood" back to the Father, we come back into a perfect relationship of love, trust and faithfulness with the Father (*redemption*).

The *fifth* word beginning with the letter *"R"* is *restoration*, which wraps up the Bible story through replenishing and *restoring* that which the enemy has stolen away from man. **We regain eternal life (*relationship* with God) by being** *reintroduced* to God the Father through His Son Jesus Christ. **We reclaim our heritage and destiny (*rulership over the earth*)** by learning that God the Father's blueprint for us has *never changed*.

*"Behold I stand at the door and knock. If anyone hears My voice and opens the door, I will come into him and dine with him, and he with Me. To him who overcomes, **I will grant to sit with Me on My throne**, as I also overcame and sat down with My Father on His throne"* (Revelation 3:20–21). (Emphasis added.) (A circular experience.)

*"And have made us kings and priests to our God; **and we shall reign on the earth**"*(Revelation 5:10). (Emphasis added.) (A circular experience.)

The five "R" words are to be taught in a *circle*.

The nature of God Himself is circular as He is the God of "Aliyah", or the ***God of return***, allowing us ***to come back*** to Him after we have fallen away, and ***thus completing the circle***. God ends what He begins. He is the Alpha and the Omega.

The nature of the Bible is also ***circular***. We reap what we sow. What we do unto others will also be done unto us. What goes around comes around.

"For with what judgment you judge, you will be judged; and with the measure you use, it will be measured back to you" (Matthew 7:2).

"Do not be deceived, God is not mocked; for whatever a man sows, that he will also reap. For he who sows to his flesh will of the flesh reap corruption, but he who sows to the Spirit will of the Spirit reap everlasting life" (Galatians 6:7–8).

"I am the Alpha and the Omega, the Beginning and the End, the First and the Last" (Revelation 22:13).

In the oldest book of the Bible, all that happened to Job is a perfect example of how everything that was taken away from Job, God eventually restored to him. First, Job had to learn who God was in order to experience complete life by trusting in Him. Job's life experience ended up being a ***circular*** one.

Our ***restoration*** phase often requires a ***lifetime*** to complete, as there are many, many lessons to be learned: lessons regarding who He is (a loving and just God), who we are to Him (His beloved children and co-heirs with Christ) and what He expects from us ("Thy will be done"). All of these lessons have eternal consequences one way or another. God cannot afford the repetition of mankind's original disastrous choice of appropriating Satan's spiritual rebellion. God cannot afford nor will He risk giving disobedient human beings their eternal resurrected glorified bodies if there's any hint of spiritual rebellion still residing within us. Doing so would allow the rebellion to continue *forever* on earth with *immortal* human rebels.

Thankfully, the Father sent His Divine Son Jesus to earth in human form to do away with the rebellious works of the devil. Jesus is the very *different* second Adam.

"For this purpose the Son of God was manifested, that He might destroy the works of the devil" (1 John 3:8). (Emphasis added.)

So what are the works of the devil that require destroying?

All sin or rebelling against the will of God has some configuration of disobedience.

For rebellion is as the sin of witchcraft, and stubbornness is as iniquity and idolatry (1 Samuel 15:23). (Emphasis added.)

Whoever commits sin also commits lawlessness, and sin is lawlessness (1 John 3:4).

The fifth chapter of Hebrews explains that even Jesus as a Son had to learn obedience to the Father:

"...though He was a Son, yet He learned obedience by the things which He suffered" (Hebrews 5:8).

If even Jesus Himself had to learn obedience to the Father, what is required of us as imperfect humans?

"And having been perfected, He became the author of eternal salvation to all who obey Him" (Hebrews 5:9). (Emphasis added.)

The poison of rebellion runs deep in our human systems, and it frequently requires different levels of surgery to remove all the toxins from our beings. Jesus is waiting for us to learn and practice "Thy will be done" in our personal lives in order to make His enemies His footstool.

"But this Man, after He had offered one sacrifice for sins forever, sat down at the right hand of God, from that time waiting till His enemies are made His footstool" (Hebrews 10:12–13).

Our continuing to rebel against God will shut down God's process of *restoring* us to our previous status as divine family members and rulers.

Obeying God is not legalism, nor is the carrying out of His will the equivalent of dead religious works. In fact, it was Jesus who instructed us *how to pray*, as contained in the only prayer He ever taught us in Matthew 6:10: "The Lord's Prayer". It is in that famous prayer that we request that our Father's "will be done". In effect, **the carrying out of God's will** is the **only** antidote to the toxicity of Satan's rebellion.

Jesus came to earth to save us from death in order that we would come alive in the Spirit by becoming righteously obedient to Our Father—in direct opposition to the rebellion.

*For **if** you live according to the flesh **you will die**; but **if by the Spirit** you put to death the deeds of the body, **you will live*** (Romans 8:13). (Emphasis added.)

*"...who Himself bore our sins in His own body on a tree, **that we, having died to sins, might live for righteousness**-by whose stripes you were healed"* (1 Peter 2:24). (Emphasis added.)

*"For this is the love of God, **that we keep His commandments**. And His commandments are not burdensome"* (1 John 5:3). (Emphasis added.)

Performing God's will in our lives is **proof** that we possess eternal life. As we saw in John 17:3 listed above, eternal life is **knowing** the only true God and Jesus Christ whom God sent. Eternal life is a personal, present tense and intimate relationship with the Godhead Himself. Eternal life is a "**Who**", not a "what".

1 John 2:3–5 explains that if we claim **to know** Jesus Christ then the **proof** of our claim will be that **we will keep** His commandments. **Doing** His will in our lives **proves** that we actually **know** Jesus Christ and in turn, **proves** that we **possess** eternal life.

Verse 4 of 1 John 2:3–5 adds that if we **claim to know** Jesus Christ and do *not* keep His commandments, then we are liars, and the truth is not found in us:

*"**Now by this we know that we know Him, if we keep His commandments**. He who says, 'I know him', and does not keep His commandments, is a liar and the truth is not in him. But whoever keeps His word, truly the love of God is perfected in him. By this we know that we are in Him"* (1 John 2:3–5). (Emphasis added.)

Restoration is a *lifetime* process. Restoration is God's university in how to *regain* our liberty from captivity. Restoration is God's university in how to *regain* our *"Eternal Life"*, which happens to be a *Person*.

"The Spirit of the Lord is upon Me, because He has anointed Me... To proclaim liberty to the captives... To set at liberty those who are oppressed..."(Luke 4:18). (Emphasis added.)

"The thief does not come except to steal, and to kill, and to destroy. I have come that they may have life, and that they may have it more abundantly" (John 10:10). (Emphasis added.)

"I am the way, the truth, and the life. No one comes to the Father except through Me" (John 14:6). (Emphasis added.)

Restoration is the completion of a *circular* process. To restore something assumes previous possession, subsequent loss and eventual restoration. In this case, the items being restored involve our previous *relationship* with the Father and our designated *rulership* over the earth.

Anywhere you look in Scripture, you will be able to locate your target topic in one of the *five circular "R"* areas. I encourage you to be a good "Berean" and verify this for yourself. You will discover how exciting this revelation is as you enable yourself to explain to anyone, believer or nonbeliever, the Bible story in simple, concise and logical language through the five "R" words in a *circular* formation.

The Bible will finally begin to make sense to many, perhaps for the first time.

Chapter 2

Why A Circle?
A Look At History

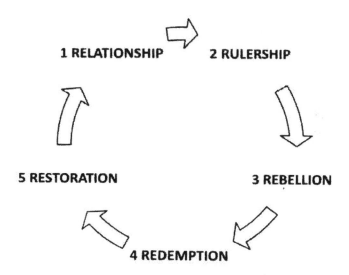

1 RELATIONSHIP   2 RULERSHIP

5 RESTORATION   3 REBELLION

4 REDEMPTION

In order to understand the present, we must first begin with understanding the past.

While preparing for a "visiting minister" sermon at a local church, I was in the process of submitting PowerPoint information to our church liaison. She informed me that she had just completed a class on Jewish culture and asked whether I was aware that Jewish language, thought and notions of time were all *circular* in nature.

You could have knocked me over with a feather.

I had been earlier curious as to why the Lord in His divine revelation to me had emphasized that the "5R" word Bible story be explained in a *circular* fashion. I decided to research her statement to explore whether there was any link between God's revelation to me and the *circular/cyclical* patterns present in Hebrew history and culture.

As I began my research, I soon learned that in many instances, Gentiles utilize a Greek, Western, *linear* way of thinking when attempting to study *cyclical/circular*, experiential, Jewish thought. As Westerners, we often default to a *linear* grid to interpret a *cyclical/circular* Hebrew foundation in the Scriptures.

I have a question: *How do you study **Hebrew cyclical/circular thought** throughout the Bible with **Greek linear** tools of interpretation without becoming confused?*

It seems like an attempt to place square pegs in round holes, resulting in a process that's incongruous at best and illogical at worst.

I began to wonder if such a contradictory analytical process could possibly explain why there is often confusion and lack of agreement amongst the many Gentile Christian denominations as to the interpretation of our Hebrew-originated Scriptures.

The first and original manifestation of what we now call "The Church" was an expression of the Hebrew mind (Knowles 1). After extensive study and research, I propose that the idea of a Hebraic, *circular/cyclical* interpretation of Scripture makes it much easier to explain the Scriptures in a straightforward manner, especially when considering the *culture*, *time*, *language* and *thought* context of the Bible's Hebrew authors. After all, at least 39 of the Bible's 40 authors were Hebrew. Shouldn't we at least attempt to explore *how* the cultural, philosophical and societal influences of their era impacted their writings?

Context is not just important. It is everything when attempting to comprehend meaning, significance and intent of the communications one is exploring. The Old Testament is written in the Hebrew language by Hebrew authors. And although the New Testament appears in the Greek language, virtually all of its authors were Hebrew who, as Jewish cultural products, were steeped in ancient Near Eastern philosophy. As Researcher Brian Knowles wrote, "The Bible in its original languages, is, humanly speaking, *a product of the Hebrew mind*" (Knowles 1). (Emphasis added.)

If you were to travel to Russia to learn the local language, culture, perspective and history, what would be your reaction if on the first day of your foreign language class, your instructor passed out textbooks labeled as Japanese dictionaries?

You get the point. It would make no sense either linguistically or culturally.

Professor Marvin Wilson in his 1989 work entitled "Our Father Abraham, Jewish Roots of the Christian Faith" explains that the context for all *the Scriptures*, including the epistles of the Apostle Paul, is that of the Jewish culture. He teaches that if we are to understand the Bible accurately, we must plug into the Hebrew background of the primeval Middle East. He adds that "the theological vocabulary and linguistic idioms behind much of the Greek New Testament are Hebraic to the very core" (Wilson 9).

Even the New Testament itself testifies to the Hebraic origins of Christianity. Paul the Apostle states that the "Gentiles are heirs *together* with Israel, *members together of one body*" (Ephesians 3:6b). (Emphasis added.) Paul explained to the

Gentile church at Corinth that the Israelites were the antecedents to the Corinthians:

"...our forefathers were all under the cloud, and...they all passed through the sea" (1 Corinthians 10:1).

"In the early church, therefore, Jew and Gentile claimed *a common spiritual ancestry* with the Hebrews of old" (Wilson 9). (Emphasis added.)

I totally ascribe to the fact that the Scriptures, as we know them, were divinely inspired (2 Timothy 3:16). I appreciate the fact that God originally appointed Jerusalem, not Athens, to be His revelatory agent (Isaiah 43:10, Isaiah 2:3).

Per the researcher Brian Knowles, over time with the progression of Church history, "something" unfortunately snatched away God's inventive Hebrew blueprint by which the movement of Yeshua (Jesus) was being constructed and replaced it with a non-Hebraic, Hellenistic, Greek-inspired one. As a result, what has been built since is at best a caricature of what was intended. Knowles ends by claiming that in many respects, it is downright contrary and antagonistic to the spirit of the original believing community (Knowles 1).

This Hellenistic, linear, Western influence has had a perverting and devastating effect on the effectiveness of the Father's circular, Hebraic blueprint witness to mankind on the earth.

Linear Greek Philosophy versus Circular Hebrew Philosophy

My own experience with Western, *linear*, Greek thinking culminated with my legal training. Most of the classes I took in law school were taught by the Socratic method, which involved utilizing systematic uncertainty to solve complicated legal scenarios. Professors would pose continual questions to students instead of answers in order to clarify issues and reveal rational solutions to legal problems in which *linear*, successive logic was valued and expected.

Years later, while working full-time as an Administrative Law Judge, I simultaneously invested eight part-time years in obtaining my bachelor's degree in theology and graduated *magna cum laude*. However, during my tenure in Bible school, I was never taught to compare the *cyclical/circular* nature of Hebrew thought/culture with the *linear*, consecutive thinking of Greek, Western thought. Rather, we were taught *systematic* theology when studying Hebrew Scripture.

Western systematic theology attempts to reduce Hebraic religious truth to statements that form an internally consistent and organized whole. Author Brad Young in his 1997 book "Paul the Jewish Theologian" *describes this form of Western thought process* that approaches theology in a *systematic straight line* by which each new idea supersedes and eliminates the previous one. He later contrasts systematic Western thought with the *"Jewish way of thinking"* illustrated with Paul the Apostle's use of *circular/cyclical* interactive concepts (Young 25, 40, 42).

Brian Knowles adds: "Intellectually we are Greeks, not Hebrews... We insist on rendering everything into logically consistent patterns, on systematizing it, on organizing it into tight, carefully reasoned theologies. We cannot live with inconsistency or contradiction... We relentlessly attempt to organize everything into manageable intellectual blocks and structures. We want all questions answered, all problems solved and all contradictions resolved" (Knowles 4).

The problem with applying *Western systematic thinking* while studying Hebrew Middle-Eastern Scripture is that this is not how the Hebrew mind works. Theologian Abraham Heschel in his 1955 work entitled "God in Search of Man" lays out the case that **Western** attempts to distill the Scriptures down to merely a set of ideas or principles would fail based on the ineffable, personal nature of Judaism's interaction with a personal God. Per Heschel, the Bible reveals a God whose series of interactions with His children produced a story of events, not just of principles (Heschel 20).

"**To the Jewish mind**, the understanding of God is **not** achieved by referring **in a Greek way** to timeless qualities of a Supreme Being, to ideas of goodness or perfection, **but rather by** sensing the living acts of His concern, to His dynamic attentiveness to man. We speak not of His goodness in general but of His compassion for the **individual** man in a **particular** setting. God's goodness is not a cosmic force but a **specific act** of compassion. We do not know it as it **is** but as it **happens**" (Heschel 21). (Emphasis added.)

"Greeks learned in order to comprehend. The Hebrews learned in order to revere" (Heschel 34).

"The ideal man of **Hebraism** is the **man of faith**. For **Hellenism**, at least as it came to ultimate philosophic expression with its two greatest philosophers, **Plato** and Aristotle, the ideal man is the **man of reason,** the philosopher who as **a spectator of all time** and existence must rise above these" (Barrett 77). For the Hebrew, "**The man of faith is the concrete man** in his wholeness. As a man of flesh and blood, Biblical man was very much bound to the earth. **Hebraism does not** raise its eyes to the universal and abstract; its vision is always on the **concrete, particular, individual man**. The **Greeks**, on the other hand, as the first thinkers in history; discovered the universal, **the abstract and timeless essences**, forms, **and Ideas**...**Plato** held **that man lives only** insofar as he lives in **the eternal**" (Barrett 77). (Emphasis added).

"*Hebraism* contains no eternal realm of essences, which *Greek philosophy* fabricated *through Plato*, as affording the *intellectual deliverance from the evil of time*. *This deliverance* would be possible only for a *detached intellect*, one who, in *Plato's* phrase, becomes a *'spectator of all time* and all existence'...*Detachment* was for the *Hebrew* an *impermissible* state of mind, *a vice* rather than a virtue" (Barrett 76). (Emphasis added.)

In a nutshell, man, *in the eyes of the Hebrew, was a man of the earth*. This earthly man's knowledge was *unlike that of the Greek*. The man of this world that God created gained his knowledge "through body and blood, bones and bowels, through trust and anger and confusion and love and fear; through his passionate adhesion in faith to the Being whom he can never intellectually know. This kind of *knowledge* a man *has only through living, not reasoning...*" (Barrett 79). (Emphasis added.)

Wilson explains that Hebrews often made use of "block logic", which is "expressed in self-contained units or blocks of thought. These blocks did not necessarily fit together in any obviously rational or harmonious pattern, particularly when one block represented the human perspective on truth and the other represented the divine" (Wilson 150). This manner of thought led to contradictions and enigmas as the two blocks stood in conflict to one another. "The Semites of Bible times did not simply think truth—they experienced truth" (Wilson 153). To the Jew, truth was as much *an encounter* as much as it was a proposition. "To the Jew, the deed was always more important than the creed... He believed that God was ultimately greater than any human attempt at systemizing truth" (Wilson 153). *Living the truth* (1 John 1:6) *and walking in the truth* (2 John 4) *for the Jew* was more important than logically examining the truth, as Greeks would tend to do (Wilson 153).

In Young's work, he, like Wilson, explains that *the Hebrew mind* viewed God in a different way from the theological, systematic thinking of the West. Westerners attempted to define God and His creation *in a linear manner* by attempting to explain and harmonize contradictions systematically.

In contrast, "The Hebrew mind was filled with wonder at the mystery of God" (Young 25). They were overcome by His majesty and His enigmatic ways. Paul the Apostle viewed God through the prism of perplexing curiosity. Paul, as a theologian, possessed a worldview that proposed theological thought operations that were *not linear* in their nature but rather were *circular* and interactively linked. Paul's thoughts (per the diagram by Young below) were connected one to another in continuous *circular* motion (Young 25, 40)

PAUL'S CONCEPTUAL THEOLOGY
Circular Thought—Not Linear

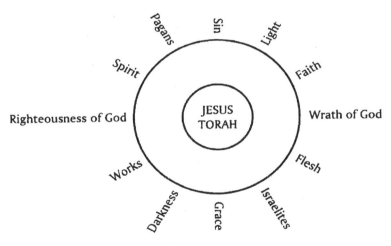

The Concepts are interactive:
in circular thought the conceptual theological ideas
are connected together in continuous motion.
The focal point is Jesus as the goal of Torah.

Greek vs. Hebrew Concepts of Time

Greek and Hebrew minds were also on opposite ends of the *time* spectrum.

The West used a *solar* calendar called the Julian calendar (named for its Roman creator Julius Caesar), later known as the Gregorian calendar as modified by Pope Gregory. The *Jews* used a **combination lunar/solar** calendar based on Genesis 1:14–16 to mark the holy days, Jubilee years, and the seven-year cyclical Shemittah year involving debt relief and allowing the land to lay fallow. The fulfillment of Jewish prophecy can only be appreciated by understanding the Hebrew Biblical calendar. As per Genesis 1:14, God specifically created the sun, moon and stars to send heavenly signals to His children at the appointed times on His calendar so we would be aware of when He wants to meet with us (Biltz 122–123).

Author Thorleif Boman in his 1960 book "Hebrew Thought Compared with Greek" explains that for the Hebrew, time determination was accomplished by means of time-rhythms rather than time lines. Their *circular/cyclical perception of time* did not necessarily refer to actual circular lines and shapes but rather to the *circular course* of life's "*rhythmic alternations* such as light and darkness, warmth and cold" (Boman 134), (Emphasis added.) seasons of the year and changes of the moon's phases. Even human life runs its rhythmic course as earth-man-earth (Boman 133–134). The Hebrews would orient themselves temporally more towards the regular changes of the moon's *alternating phases* rather than the actual circular movement of the sun. This *rhythmic alternation concept* originates with the Hebrew stem word *dor*, which may be derived from the same root as *dur*, which means a "*circular course, circle*" (Boman 134) whose *rhythms* can be seen, such as in the Jewish circle dances of unbroken unity. For the Hebrew, their great reality consists of an eternally ongoing *circular/cyclical rhythmic repetition* formed by a beginning, a continuation and concluding with a return to the beginning once again (Boman 133–135).

In the book of Ecclesiastes, one can see references to the *circular/cyclical* pictures of *nature's* functions observing the sun, wind, rivers and the sea operating in their *alternating rhythmic cycles*:

*What profit has a man from all his labor in which he toils under the sun? One generation passes away, and another generation comes; but the earth abides forever. The sun also rises, and the sun goes down, and hastens to the place where it arose. The wind goes toward the south, **and turns around** to the north; The wind whirls about continually, **and comes again on its circuit**. All the rivers run into the sea, yet the sea is not full; to the place from which the rivers come, **There they return again**"* (Ecclesiastes 1:3–7). (Emphasis added.)

Even human life is observed as a *cycle* (Boman 135).

"Naked I came from my mother's womb, and naked I shall return there. The Lord gave, and the Lord has taken away; Blessed be the name of the Lord" (Job 1:21).

Researcher Brian Knowles in his article *The Hebrew vs. The Western Mind* explains that **the Western mind** functions in terms of "prophetic timetables" in which the concept of time equates to *sequential points* on a forward-facing timeline. Each event in time is new, thereby creating a perspective that time is *linear*. He concludes that *Westerners* desire to have their "prophetic timetables" end in nicely arranged units of time and space (Knowles 2,3).

For the Jew, the *sequential* order in which God acts is of no great concern. The main point is that God will carry out what

He intends to do in His own time. "The day of the Lord" for the Hebrew is the day or time when the Lord acts. The sequential order of when the Lord acts is of no importance for the Jew. All that is important is to know that the Lord *will* act (Knowles 2).

For the Greek, time is primarily *spatial* and is represented as a *straight line* upon which we Westerners stand, looking forward to the future before us and with our past behind us. All present, past and future verb tenses are expressed by and through points on a straight line, which can be without limit. This *linear* thinking stemmed from ancient Greek philosophies, namely those influenced by the Greek thinkers Aristotle and Plato (Boman 124–127).

"Contempt for time seems to be characteristic of human thoughts almost everywhere...*to the Greek mind*, time compared with eternity appears empty, irrelevant and essentially unreal. Things that happen in history are of little significance; only the timeless is truly relevant...It was the glory of Greece to have discovered the idea of cosmos, the world of space...Time for the non-prophetic man is the dark destroyer, and history is at bottom meaningless, a monotonous repetition of hatred, bloodshed and armistice" (Heschel 205–206). (Emphasis added.)

According to Boman, **Aristotle** analyzed time from a natural science viewpoint, stating that *successive* movements on the image of a line represent time. The line may be *circular* to indicate objective, physical or astronomical chronometry (the movement of the sun, moon and the stars), or it may be straight, which is required to define grammatical time like the past, present or future.

Plato analyzed time from a religious viewpoint, focusing primarily on eternity. His concept of time was mostly related to the category of inner life, events and history. He believed that consciousness is primary and physical movement secondary. Both philosophers agreed that time is inferior to space and therefore, is viewed as destructive rather than constructive. As a result, everything deteriorates under the continuing pressure of time. Thus, time as understood by the Greeks was viewed with contempt (Boman 124–128).

In contrast, for the Hebrew, time is not determined by its passing but rather by its ***content***. "The heavenly luminaries emit differing intensities of light and warmth, and in that way, they define time. The time when the sun is the dominant light-and warmth-giver is the day, but the time when the moon is the dominant light and together with the stars, gives illumination is night (Genesis 1:16)" (Boman 131).

One of the best examples of how ***Hebrews*** would describe ***time*** by its ***content*** can be found in the third chapter in the book of Ecclesiastes:

To everything there is a season, A time for every purpose under heaven:
A time to be born, And a time to die;
A time to plant, And a time to pluck what is planted;
A time to kill, A time to heal; A time to break down, And a time to build up;
A time to weep, And a time to laugh; A time to mourn, And a time to dance;
A time to cast away stones, And a time to gather stones;
A time to embrace And the time to refrain from embracing;
A time to gain, And a time to lose; A time to keep, And a time to throw away;
A time to tear, And a time to sew; A time to keep silence, And a time to speak;
A time to love, A time to hate; A time of war, And a time of peace (Ecclesiastes 3:1–8).

"...It was the achievement of Israel to have experienced history, the world of *time. Judaism* claims that time is exceedingly relevant. Elusive as it may be, it is pregnant with the seeds of eternity. Significant to God and decisive for the destiny of man are the things that happen in time and in history. Biblical history is the triumph of time over space... History is the supreme witness for God. We must remember that God is involved in our doings, that meaning is given not only in the timeless but primarily in the timely, in that task given here and now...For time is but a little lower than eternity, and history is a drama in which both man and God have a stake" (Heschel 206–207) (Emphasis added).

Can you now see how the Hebrew explained time by its content?

The verses cited above in Ecclesiastes chapter 3 and the quotes from Professor Heschel delineate seasons or time frames that describe real human emotions and *experiences* that would often occur *cyclically* in peoples' lives. The *Hebrew* point of view of time *being described by its content* assists us Westerners in understanding how the Hebrew *temporally* engaged the world *experientially*.

Greek versus Hebrew Opinions on Matter

Hebrews and Greeks also had drastically varying viewpoints in regards to tangible matter—our physical bodies along with the physical earth that we inhabit and its role in our lives.

One of the most influential of the ancient Greek philosophies, Platonism, originated with the philosopher Plato who viewed humans, their lives and their world in a dualistic manner. Plato's bifurcated view eventually influenced much of the ancient heretical belief of Gnosticism, which taught that all matter, including the human body, was essentially evil.

Gnostics taught that Jesus could not be God in flesh because the body as matter was evil. Likewise, the human body was considered a defective and obsolete place of confinement for the imprisonment of man's *"pure"* immortal soul. Simply put: Spirit was good. Matter was evil.

Platonism purported that the earth was one element of *two* separate worlds. The earth belonged to the tangible, material world that differed from the intangible, spiritual world, and neither world was in sync nor compatible with the other. *The material, earthly world* was deemed *inferior* when contrasted with the *celestial, perfect, spiritual world*. Platonists and Gnostics believed that the defective earth was not something to be enjoyed but rather was to be shunned and later cast off, and it was certainly not to be considered man's permanent home. Spiritual maturity occurred only by escaping through asceticism—self-isolation, self-deprivation of possessions and self-imposition of hardships—practices believed to elevate the individual to a higher level of godliness. The human body for Plato served as a defective prison for the soul. *Freedom/salvation did not occur until physical death*, which allowed the soul to finally jettison one's corrupt body and the fallen physical world to ascend to the *ethereal perfection* of the *spiritual world* beyond (Wilson 168).

Gnosticism had its early impacts on the Church, which can be seen with Paul the Apostle addressing the practice of asceticism in Colossians 2:20–23 and in the first epistle of the Apostle John when he addresses the Gnostic challenge that Jesus as God was not raised in the flesh. Gnosticism even influenced early Christian theology through the ascetic practices and Platonic philosophies of "the father of Christian theology": Origen of Alexandria (Wilson 168-169).

By contrast, *the Hebrew mind* saw God the Father's earthly creation *as something good* for mankind, despite understanding the earth had fallen due to Satan's invading rebellion (Isaiah 14:12 et seq.). "The Hebrew Bible is clearly a worldly book" (Wilson 170). Hebrews understood that man's ultimate goal was **not** to escape the material world by shirking his God-given responsibility to establish God's order and government on earth. They believed that rather than escape the earth, man was to reestablish God's civilization on it. They understood that **redeeming** the fallen world requires **a sovereign intervention on behalf of the Creator** to bring **salvation** in the form of **liberation** from the hands of their enemies (Luke 1:67–79). Interaction with God brought **deliverance from one's enemies** and **restored relationship** with God along with His outpouring of blessings on His children. Unlike the Greeks, Hebrew concepts of redemption, reconciliation, **salvation,** liberty and deliverance **involved being rescued from their enemies** and **being brought back to their God** (a **circular** concept) as opposed to being saved to escape the earth by being ushered away to a celestial place.

Now his father **Zacharias** *was filled with the Holy Spirit, and prophesied, saying: "Blessed is the Lord God* **of Israel***, for He has visited* **and redeemed His people***, and has raised up a* **horn of salvation** *for us…* **That we should be saved** *from our* **enemies** *and from the hand of* **all who hate us***…To grant us that we,* **being delivered from the hand of our enemies***,* **Might serve Him** *without fear, In holiness and righteousness before Him all the days of our life* (Luke 1:67–69,71,74–75). (Emphasis added.)

For if when we were enemies **we were reconciled to God through the death of His Son***, much more, having been reconciled, we shall be saved by His life* (Romans 5:10). (Emphasis added.)

Now all things are of God, **Who has reconciled us to Himself through Jesus Christ**, *and has given us the ministry of reconciliation,* (2 Corinthians 5:18). (Emphasis added.)

For Christ also suffered once for sins, the just for the unjust, **that He might bring us to God**, *being put to death in the flesh but made alive by the Spirit,* (1 Peter 3:18). (Emphasis added.)

John the Baptist was the first man to announce that God's heavenly government would reinvade the fallen earth by targeting Lucifer and his government of rebellion. Lucifer's rebellious government was about to be replaced. Later, God in the divine form of man, Jesus of Nazareth, confirmed it.

In those days John the Baptist came preaching in the wilderness of Judea, and saying, "Repent, for the kingdom of heaven is at hand!" (Matthew 3:1–2).

"In this manner, therefore, pray: Our Father in heaven, Hallowed be Your name. **Your kingdom come. Your will be done on earth** *as it is in heaven* (Matthew 6:9–10). (Emphasis added.)

Circular/Cyclical Patterns in Creation

God Himself has *created* in **circular/cyclical** *patterns* and *designs* that can be observed by just living in His world.

As we look around the physical universe we see that stars have life cycles and that the ocean tides ebb and flow cyclically two times a day. We experience the cyclical changing of the seasons each year. We observe the moon's monthly cyclical phases along with the annual changes of the sun. All are repeated over and over.

Cycles govern the affairs of mankind from the rise and fall of empires to the booms and busts of economies, currencies, and commodities. (Check out Edward S. Dewey of the President Herbert Hoover Administration.)

As human beings, we are made in God's image.

Then God said, "Let Us make man in Our image, according to Our likeness..." (Genesis 1:26).

Cyclical/circular patterns are reflected in human physiology through **alternating rhythmic patterns** of electrochemical feedback *loops* called cybernetics. Dr. Caroline Leaf explains that our human nervous systems are comprised of these always-in-motion electrochemical systems and **circular** *feedback loops* (Leaf 24–25).

Even a doctor or nurse listening through a stethoscope to the *rhythmic* sounds of the human heart hears a strong beat followed by a weak beat then again a strong beat with the *same* **repetitious alternating patterns** of the heart's diastolic and systolic functions.

In terms of earth science, **observable cycles** are everywhere. Chickens come home to roost (so do the swallows annually at the California Mission in San Juan Capistrano), the California grey whales **cyclically migrate** every year between Baja California and Alaska, precipitation evaporates **back** into the atmosphere from whence it earlier fell as rain and electricity always seeks *to **return back*** to its ground source.

On a philosophical level, we're all familiar with the adages "what goes around comes around" and "those who cannot remember the past are condemned to repeat it."

In Christian doctrine, the Holy Spirit speaks in terms of *reaping what we sow* in Paul's letter to the Galatians:

"Do not be deceived, God is not mocked; for whatever a man sows, that he will also reap" (Galatians 6:7).

Jesus taught that as we judge, we will also be judged by the same measure. He also taught we are to treat others as we wish to be treated (Matthew 7:12).

The Circular Bible Account

God is a God of "Aliyah".

The term "aliyah" has come to mean "the return" of the Jews of the Diaspora (Jewish dispersion after Roman conquest and destruction of the Second Temple in 70 A.D.) back to their promised homeland of Israel. Several returns to the Jewish homeland in recent history have taken place, beginning in the late 19th century and continuing on into the 20th century. Jews returned in waves back to their homeland under the British Mandate before as well as after World War II. After the United Nations officially recognized Israel as a sovereign nation in 1948, waves of Jewish migrations from the Soviet Union during the 1980's continued despite internal Soviet resistance. Even Jews from Ethiopia made "aliyah" back to the homeland of Israel during this time.

The Hebrew prophets Isaiah, Jeremiah, Zechariah and Ezekiel, to name a few, had prophesied about many of these homeland returns.

*It shall come to pass in that day that **the Lord shall set His hand again the second time to recover the remnant of His people** who are left, from Assyria and Egypt, from Pathros and Cush, from Elam and Shinar, from Hamath and the islands of* *the sea. He will set up a banner for the nations, **and will assemble the outcasts of Israel**, and **gather together the dispersed** of Judah from the four corners of the earth* (Isaiah 11:11–12). (Emphasis added.)

*"Therefore behold, the days are coming," says the Lord, "that it shall no more be said, the Lord lives who brought up the children of Israel from the land of Egypt,' "but, 'The **Lord lives who brought up the children of Israel from the land of the north and from all the lands where He had driven them.' For I will bring them back into their land which I gave to their fathers"*** (Jeremiah 16:14–15). (Emphasis added.)

This God of Aliyah can be seen over and over by observing the Hebrew historical experience in the Old Testament. This *cyclical/circular* trend occurs throughout the historical accounts of the Israelites, beginning in the oldest book of the Bible, Job (who prospered, lost everything, then prospered again at a much greater level), then in the Pentateuch (the first five books of the Bible) and on into the Historical and Prophetical books.

The Hebrew interaction with their Creator brought on *a circular/cyclical* experiential perspective as to the nature and character of this God of Aliyah—this God of the return and this God of second chances. We see these *circular* pattern experiences with the Jews that deal with *God's initial blessings then* often followed by the *Hebrew nation's subsequent fall from grace.* This resulted in *warnings from prophets* followed by *divine judgments*, which ultimately led to *repentance.* Eventual *reconciliation* resulted in the *full circle renewal* and *restoration of blessings* from God. The Bible's numerous *circular/cyclical* patterns are apparent throughout the extensive accounts of God's dealings with the children of Israel that reveal His loving, parental and longsuffering character.

One such account is that of Gideon placing a fleece before God to inquire about his role as a "mighty man of valor" and deliverer of Israel (Judges 5–6). We see in the *beginning* of the account in Judges chapter 5 that the land of Israel finally **had experienced rest** for a 40-year period of time. After God's 40-year blessing on the Hebrew nation, the book of Judges explains that the children of Israel **did evil** in the sight of the Lord (***apostasy/fall from grace***). In Judges chapter 6, the Lord sent a prophet to Israel to warn them that they had not obeyed the voice of the Lord.

Judgment follows when the Lord delivered Israel into the hand of Midian for seven years. Due to the victories of the Midianites, the children of Israel were forced to hide out in dens, caves and in the mountains. Israel's produce of the earth was destroyed, leaving no sustenance for the children of God. As impoverishment took over, the children of Israel cried out to the Lord in ***repentance***.

The Lord provided triumph and liberty to Israel through the miraculous military victory of Gideon's 300 over the 135,000 Midianites (***deliverance***). ***Reconciliation*** and ***blessings*** then ***returned*** to the children of Israel ***as they returned*** to God.

We observe again a ***circular/cyclical*** experience.

*Then the men of Israel said to Gideon, "Rule over us, both you and your son, and your grandson also; for you to have delivered us from the hand of Midian." But Gideon said to them, "I will not rule over you, nor shall my son rule over you; the **Lord shall rule over you**"* (Judges 8:22–23). (Emphasis added.) (**Reconciliation.**)

*Thus Midian was subdued before the children of Israel, so that they lifted their heads no more. And the country **was quiet** for*

40 years in the days of Gideon (Judges 8:28). (Emphasis added.) (**Return of Blessings.**)

An additional Old Testament *circular/cyclical* pattern can also be observed with the fall of the two remaining Hebrew southern tribes of Judah to King Nebuchadnezzar, ruler of Babylon.

Prior to the fall of the southern kingdom of Judah to the Babylonian invaders, two righteous kings named Hezekiah and Josiah set out to remove the mixture of Canaanite pagan influence with the Hebrew worship of God. The high places of pagan worship were destroyed, and the purity of God worship was restored. God blessed the kingdom of Judah for approximately 100 years.

Unfortunately, the two righteous kings were replaced by the Kings Ahaz and Manasseh, who not only allowed worship of Canaanite gods, but also went so far as to include the additional worship to the ravenous god of Moloch to whom the Jews would sacrifice their own children. (*Apostasy*.) Despite *warnings* from the prophets Isaiah, Jeremiah and Micah, Judah's renunciation of the Father's instructions relentlessly continued.

*"But this is what I commanded them, saying, '**Obey My voice, and I will be your God**, and you shall be My people. **And walk in all the ways that I have commanded you**, that **it may be well** with you.'*

*"**Yet they did not obey** or incline their ear, but followed the counsels and the dictates of their evil hearts, and went backward and not forward. (**Apostasy**.)*

*"Since the day that your fathers came out of the land of Egypt until this day, I have even sent to you all My servants the prophets, (**warnings**) daily rising up early and sending them.*

"For the children of Judah have done evil in My sight," says the Lord. "They have set their abominations in the house which is called by My name, to pollute it.

"The corpses of this people will be food for the birds of the heaven and for the beasts of the earth. And no one will frighten them away. "Then I will cause to cease from the cities of Judah and from the streets of Jerusalem the voice of mirth and the voice of gladness, the voice of the bridegroom and the voice of the bride. For the land shall be desolate. (**Judgment.**) (Jeremiah 7:23–28, 30–31, 33–34.) (Emphasis and key words added.)

Judgment did eventually fall on the remaining kingdom of Judah. The Temple was destroyed and Jerusalem set ablaze; its walls flattened. The inhabitants were vanquished and exiled to Babylon where they would remain captive for 70 years.

The prophet Jeremiah remained behind with the destruction of Jerusalem and from there wrote a letter (Jeremiah 29) to all the exiles carried away to Babylon. His letter was one of hope and renewal. The idea of God being a God of "Aliyah" is expressed in several ways including themes of *repentance*, *return* to the land and to the Father, *restoration* and new dimensions of *relationship*.

Thus says the Lord of hosts, the God of Israel, to all who are carried away captive, whom I have caused to be carried away from Jerusalem to Babylon (Jeremiah 29:4).

For thus says the Lord: after 70 years are completed at Babylon, I will visit you and perform My good word toward *you, and cause you to return (**return**) to this place. For I know the thoughts that I think toward you, says the Lord, thoughts of peace and not of evil, to give you a future and a hope (**restoration**). Then you will call upon me and go and pray to Me, and I will listen to you. And you will seek Me and find Me, when you search for Me with all your heart. I will be found by you, (**relationship**) says the Lord, and I will bring you back (**return**) from your captivity; I will gather you from all the nations and from all the places where I have driven you, says the Lord, and I will bring you to the place from which I caused you to be carried away captive.* (Jeremiah 29:4,10–14). (Emphasis and key words added.)*

*'For behold, the days are coming, says the Lord, 'that I will **bring back** from captivity my people Israel and Judah,' says the Lord. 'And I will cause them **to return** to the land that I gave to their fathers, and they shall possess it' "*(**Return.**) (Jeremiah 30:3). (Emphasis and key word added.)

'Therefore all those who devour you shall be devoured; and all your adversaries, every one of them, shall go into captivity; Those who plunder you shall become plunder, and all who prey upon you I will make a prey (**Deliverance.**) (Jeremiah 30:16). (Emphasis and keyword added.)

*For I will **restore** health to you and heal you of your wounds,' says the Lord, because they called you an outcast saying: "This is Zion; no one seeks her"'* (**Restoration.**) (Jeremiah 30:17). (Emphasis and keyword added.)

We see this *circular/ cyclical* pattern of *redemption* and *restoration* continue on into the *New Testament* message in the parable of the Prodigal Son. The son's loving father is one who refuses to stop looking for the prodigal son's eventual *physical return* (aliyah) to have *restored relationship* with his father, with his family and with his inheritance.

Additionally, we see in the *New Testament* that even *the return of Jesus back* to His Father from the earth was *circular*.

Our Father God continues to yearn for *our personal return back to Him and back to our earthly home designated for us*. This revelation includes the discovery that our Divine Father is a God of second chances *for redemption* and *restoration* of ruptured relationship due to our immature, rebellious and disobedient choices. Our Father's acceptance of us completes the *circle back* to His perfect original blueprint.

Alternate Viewpoints to the Circular Account

In my research for this work, I learned that two of the eminent authors I studied offered what *appeared* initially to be an alternative view to my theory that the Bible account of God's blueprint for mankind is indeed a Hebrew cycle/circle rather than a Greek/Western linear straight line.

In his 1998 book "The Gifts of the Jews" author Thomas Cahill explained that the local pagan concept of time and destination in the regions referred to as Sumer (modern-day Iraq) involved a hopeless, monotonous, futureless, frustrating repetition of a "*wheel*-like" turning of the life-death cycle. In essence, the sum of life consisted of "birth, copulation and personal death" (Cahill 47) only to repeat itself with subsequent generations. Missing was a purpose to the endless cyclical repetition. Insatiable pagan gods were to receive various offerings of sacrifices, including human, without producing any significant goal or hope to end the drudgery of the pagan human condition. Death actually served as a release from the seemingly never-ending replay of previous experiences (Cahill 47).

According to authors Cahill and Wilson, the counterbalance Hebrew experience beginning with Abraham and continuing with Moses, produced a unique launching of the Jewish people

34

along a *linear* trajectory towards the specific goals of personal relationship with the Almighty God. In their analyses of the newly linear travels of the Hebrews (from Ur to Canaan and from Egypt to Canaan), they conclude that the Hebrew historical experience is not compatible with the pagan, interminable, futile, circular "wheel" of the Sumerians (Cahill 131–132; Wilson 161).

My take on all this is that their interpretation is apt so long as the authors are not considering the original blueprint of the Creator expressed in Genesis chapter 1. Ironically, the authors themselves admit to a circular, cyclical pattern of the Hebrew historical, experiential reality.

For example, Wilson maintains, "In Hebrew thought the essence of true godliness *is tied primarily to a relationship, not to a creed*. The Lord is the God of Israel, and Israel is the people of God (Leviticus 26:12–13, et seq.)". Here is the leitmotif of Biblical theology. The Torah gives direction to Israel on how to *relate* to the Creator, His people and His world. Sin *ruptures* that relationship, but *repentance* brings forgiveness and *restoration to fellowship*" (Wilson 138). (Emphasis added.)

Thus, it appears that Wilson includes four of the five elements of the "5-R" blueprint circle in his description of the Hebrew perspective of biblical theology. The elements appear to form *a loop or a circle*. Restoration *returns* mankind *back* to the beginning of the *circle*, i.e. the *relationship* between the Creator and man.

Another example illustrating Wilson's proposal of a Hebrew *linear* concept of time: "Rather, in sharp distinction, the Hebrew view of time in history was essentially linear, durative, and progressive. In short, it was going somewhere; it was en route to a goal, a glorious climax at the end of this age" (Wilson 161).

However, in his very next statement, Wilson *again* seems to argue for a *circular return* of Godly rule over the earth with the expunging of evil, *redemption* of the righteous from sin and *restoration* of God's original blueprint design in Genesis: "The consummation of history in the age to come will see nature transformed through the *removal* of *evil from the earth*. 'On that day' God will judge the wicked and *redeem* the righteous, and 'the *Lord will be king* over the whole earth'" (Zechariah 14:9) (*Restoration*.) (Wilson 161–162). (Emphasis and key word added.)

The author Thomas Cahill in his 1998 work "The Gifts of the Jews" emphasizes the distinction of what he contends to be a seemingly different historical, *linear* path of the Jews when contrasted with the "*wheel*"-like (circular/cyclical) pagan societies of the region of Sumer and its surrounding areas.

Again, I contend that if Mr. Cahill had considered the picture of God's original blueprint design laid out in the first two chapters of Genesis, the author may very well have qualified his *linear* Hebrew path assertion to be truly *"aliyah"* in its nature, *i.e. cyclical/circular*.

The basis for my contention lies with Cahill's conclusions stating that the *repentant* Jewish exiles not only *returned* to their homeland after 70 years of Babylonian captivity, but were also confronted with the prospect of a *personal return* to their Creator who was not interested in blood and smoke sacrifices, but rather was seeking a personal, dedicated *relationship* (Cahill 222, 226). Thus again, Cahill sees a *circular* experience in light of the Father's original blueprint illustrated in Genesis 1–2.

The prophet Micah and later Ezekiel and Jeremiah delivered God's *personal return* invitation to the Jews:

He has shown you, O man, what is good; And what does the Lord require of you But to do justly, To love mercy, And to walk humbly with your God? (Micah 6:8).

*"Therefore say, 'Thus says the Lord God: "I will gather you from the peoples, assemble you from the countries where you have been scattered, **and I will give you the land of Israel.**"...* **(Restoration)** *"Then I will give them one heart, and I will put a new spirit within them, and **take the stony heart out of their flesh, and give them a heart of flesh,** "that they may walk in My statutes and keep My judgments and do them; **and they shall be My people, and I will be their God** (**Relationship.**)* (Ezekiel 11:17, 19–20). (Emphasis and parenthetical words added.)

*"Set up signposts, Make landmarks; **Set your heart** toward the highway, the way in which you went. **Turn back,** O virgin of Israel, **Turn back to these your cities.** (**Restoration.**)*

"And it shall come to pass, that as I have watched over them to pluck up, to break down, to throw down, to destroy, and to afflict, so I will watch over them to build and to plant, says the Lord.

*"Behold, the days are coming says the Lord, when I will make a new covenant with the house of Israel and with the house of Judah, ... "But this is the covenant that I will make with the house of Israel after those days, says the Lord: I will put my law in their minds, **and write it on their hearts; and I will be their God, and they shall be My people. (Relationship.)***** (Jeremiah 31:21, 28, 31, 33). (Emphasis and parenthetical words added.)

The first two chapters of Genesis contain the first two "R"s of **Relationship** and **Rulership** of the blueprint circle. You can observe here the Hebrews *returning* to God's perfect creation blueprint of *heart-felt relationship* between the Father Creator and His children. You can also see God's provision to His children *returning* them to their destiny *of ruling the earth*, as earlier promised by the Father in the first two chapters of the book of Genesis.

Cahill's description of the Jews *returning* from the Babylonian exile as errant children *back* to their Creator Father to receive their new *relational* hearts of flesh on which God's law would be inscribed, is actually demonstrative of the *circular* nature of the Bible account of the "5-R" circle that I propose. In addition, the post-Babylonian exile reveals *redemption* and *restoration* of the Jews *back* to their cities and land where they had earlier lived. The Hebrews again experienced the *circular/cyclical* "**Aliyah**" nature of their Father God.

Contrary to the assertion of the author, I maintain that their journey was *not* linear. Rather, it was a *circular* journey *back* to their God and *back* to their homeland. The Jews experienced *restoration* of the first two blueprint "R's" (relationship and rulership) of the "5-R" circle account (Cahill 225–229).

Even Jesus' return back to His Father from earth was *circular*.

"Most assuredly, I say to you, he who believes in Me, the works that I do he will do also; and greater works than these he will do, because I go to My Father (John 14:12). (Emphasis added.)

Jesus' second coming back to earth will also be a *circular* event.

"I will declare the decree: The Lord has said to Me, 'You are My Son, Today I have begotten You. Ask of Me, and I will give

*You The nations for Your inheritance, **And the ends of the earth for Your possession**. You shall break them with a rod of iron; You shall dash them to pieces like a potter's vessel'* "(Psalms 2:7–9).

*"Therefore you also be ready, for the **Son of Man is coming** at an hour you cannot expect"* (Matthew 24:44).

*"**When the Son of Man comes in His glory**, and all the holy angels with Him, then He will sit on the throne of His glory. "All the nations will be gathered before Him, and He will separate them one from another, as a shepherd divides his sheep from the goats. "And He will set the sheep on His right hand, but the goats on the left. "Then the King will say to those on His right hand, 'Come, you blessed of My Father, inherit the kingdom prepared for you from the foundation of the world...*(Matthew 25: 31-34). (Emphasis added.)

Does it really **make any difference** whether the Bible account is *circular* or *linear* in scope and design? Is there any *practical* impact on people, or is this just a theoretical theological discussion about how many angels can stand on the head of a pin?

God's Lost Army

Many of us in the Gentile Church today do not even realize we are engaged in spiritual warfare. Our present day ignorance results in severe earthly and eternal consequences. We are often oblivious to the fact that we have been enlisted as soldiers (2 Timothy 2:3–4). We are also oblivious to the fact that we are in the middle of a battle against the chief rebel and liar, Satan, who, as the accuser and usurper, plans to maintain and enlarge his kingdom government on earth.

"And from the days of John the Baptist until now the kingdom of heaven suffers violence, and the violent take it by force (Matthew 11:12).

One of our kingdom roles is to be effective soldiers of Jesus Christ, which involves learning how to engage in spiritual warfare strategy and tactics. We have had several hymns and worship songs in our churches that describe our role in this spiritual warfare as members of God's army.

However, I have some additional questions:

1) Would it be a problem if a designated army did not know the goal or the target of its particular mission?
2) Would it be a problem if this army did not know the ultimate destination toward which it was traveling?
3) Would it be a problem if the army were not even aware that it was involved in spiritual battles and warfare?

In my book "God Has a Problem (On His Hands)", I explain that during war, a key element in defeating your enemy is distracting them from their goal. If the eyes of the opposition's soldiers are not focused on the correct target, the result is distraction, confusion and most likely losing the war. However, the same principle also applies to us. If we are not focused *on the designated goals as determined by our General, Jesus the Lord of Hosts*, then we will also suffer defeat.

"Who is this King of glory? The Lord strong and mighty, the Lord might in battle" (Psalm 24:8).

"My people are destroyed for lack of knowledge..." (Hosea 4:6).

An example of the above is illustrated in the World War II movie "The Longest Day", which portrays the impact of what

40

occurs when the enemy successfully deceives the invading army simply by partially turning around a road sign. The deceptive twisting of the sign results in it pointing in the entirely wrong direction.

The scene portrays U.S. 101st and 82nd Airborne Unit paratroopers in the predawn hours of the 1944 invasion of Normandy. The goal was to land behind enemy lines at night to secure vital targets in preparation for the D-Day beach landings. One particular target included the French town of Ste. Mere Eglise. This was the town the American paratroopers had been ordered to take and hold in order to prevent Nazi tank reinforcements from reaching the beaches at Normandy where landing Allied infantry would be slaughtered. Securing that town was vital to the success of the invasion, and thousands of lives weighed in the balance.

In the film, John Wayne portrays a lieutenant colonel, who despite breaking his leg while parachuting behind enemy lines the previous night, is still able to discern by looking at his compass and map that something was awry with the road sign in the background. He repeats over and over again, "North by east, north by east. Ste. Mere Eglise is that way. Somebody must have turned that sign around." Holding his compass in his left hand, he points with his right, indicating the exact opposite direction of the road sign in the background with the name "Ste. Mere Eglise." The colonel is exasperated while addressing a paratrooper captain who should have known better. Again with frustration in his voice, the colonel addresses the captain by asking, "Doesn't anyone in this outfit look at a compass besides me?"

His anger was justified. The answer to his question was "no". The entire Army Airborne Paratrooper Unit was headed in the wrong direction because no one bothered to consult their compass or interpret their map. The lower rank officers had relied on a sabotaged road sign for direction. The colonel commands that the twisted road sign be knocked down, and the entire paratrooper regiment changes course in the opposite direction of the sign. But for the colonel's discernment, the military mistake that was about to occur could have caused additional severe loss of life to the American, British, French and Canadian soldiers landing on the beaches of Normandy.

Much like the soldiers in the film, the Lord's Army today has also become lost and directionless because we did not check our Holy Spirit compass to interpret our map of God's written word. In this case, Satan sabotaged the road sign by turning it around and changing the original *circular* arrow on the sign into a *linear* arrow.

Our enemy sabotaged the road sign through the insidious influence of Greek Platonic philosophy and Gnosticism. This heretical thought in turn began to creep into early Christian theology as the Hebrew Gospel became more and more "Hellenized" (Greek-like) after the Jews were dispersed from Israel in 70 A.D. As the Hebrew gospel became more geographically and culturally separated from its original Hebrew roots, the more distorted (and consequently more linear) it became. Unfortunately, many in God's Army today do not even bother to check their map of Scripture or their compass of the Holy Spirit along their journeys and continue to follow the *linear* arrow of the sabotaged sign.

So how did Satan take the Army of God's eyes off the target? How did he so aptly twist the road sign to sabotage our course of direction? He successfully distracted God's children by confusing us regarding God's ultimate goal for our *circular* Christian redemption.

Question: Do you think it makes any difference in our Christian walk whether we understand what God's goal and targets are and whether He thinks in a *circular* or a *linear* fashion when describing His goals? Just how many lives may weigh in the balance?

Is the Goal of the Christian Redemption Circular or Linear?

God the Father selected a Middle Eastern, Hebrew culture/nation, not a Greek or Roman culture through which to reveal Himself, which consist of two very different worlds (Isaiah 43:10–15). Our Greek, Western, *linear* thinking is actually leading us away from *the real goals* of the Hebrew, *circular* blueprint plan. Our Western way of Platonic escapist thinking and teaching is taking us on an erroneous trajectory out into the spiritual atmosphere *by overemphasizing* Heaven as our permanent home, while we permanently leave the earth and its nations behind as lost causes. Satan could not be happier. (See the Second Temptation of Christ in Luke 4:5–8.)

How is it that we bought into the misdirection of Greek-style Platonic dualism and Gnosticism that overemphasizes the elevation of a "spiritual" place *over God's goal* of restored personal relationship and our restored earthly inheritance? Did God wake up one morning to discover that He had made a terrible mistake? Did He ever throw out His *original blueprint* in order to resort to a "Plan B"? Has He ever changed His mind about His original plan of restoring relationship *in a circular fashion* with us, and having mankind rule and reign over the earth under the headship of Yeshua? Did we as mortals invent a goal of God that isn't found in Scripture? Shouldn't we have Biblical backup for what we believe?

I am still searching for those "Plan B" verses.

The truth is that God has never forgotten the earth and its inhabitants. Nor has He forgotten His *original blueprint* in

Genesis. He has **never** changed His mind from when He declared on the 6th day *that everything He created* was *"very good"* (Genesis 1:31). God's blueprint allows us to understand that instead of going in a *linear* fashion to Heaven "as God's goal" to forever exist as disembodied spirits, we discover that in reality, we the saints and the heavenly Holy City, the New Jerusalem, *are returning back to the earth* (Revelation 21:1–2). There will be a convergence of the Kingdom of Heaven returning to the earth. This will fulfill God's *circular* plan of replacing Satan's government of rebellion on the earth with God's Kingdom government of love and obedience on the earth.

*"Your kingdom come. Your will be done **on earth** as it is in heaven"* (Matthew 6:10). (Emphasis added.)

God's *circular* plan includes our reconciliation with Him as our Father and our future bodily resurrection and return to the earth to rule its nations with Jesus in charge as King of Kings and Lord of Lords.

*And they sang a new song, saying:" You are worthy to take the scroll, and to open its seals; **for You were slain, and have redeemed us to God by Your blood** Out of every tribe and tongue and people and nation, **And have made us kings and priests to our God; and we shall reign on the earth"** (Revelation 5: 9–10). (Emphasis added.)

We *as soldiers* of Christ *need to understand* the Father's goal of *returning* us to His perfect blueprint. That will only happen when we start to carefully read our "maps" (the Word of God) while consulting our "compasses" (requesting the sending of The Holy Spirit) to comprehend *the objective* of our mission. Our Father intends to reconcile us *back to Him through* His Son, Jesus Christ, our Messiah (a *circular* experience). The *main* reason Jesus came to earth was to *restore* our access to an intimate relationship *with our Father*.

For Christ also suffered once for sins, the just for the unjust, that He might bring us to God, being put to death in the flesh but made alive by the Spirit (1 Peter 3:18). (Emphasis added.)

We didn't lose Heaven in the Garden. *We lost* our *relationship* with God.

You can't restore something that you didn't lose in the first place. *We lost God, not Heaven*.

One of the issues we have to decide is whether or not living *forever* in Heaven operates as God's goal of the Christian redemption. It's important to note at this stage that I am very pro-Heaven. When I die, I want to go Heaven, which is the marvelous place based on Christ's description of it as paradise to the thief on the cross. In the third Heaven, Paul the Apostle experienced and observed things that were beyond his ability to explain in words. I do not wish to steal away anyone's Heaven. It is part of the package of redemption.

However, I have not found a single verse in the Bible that describes Heaven *as the goal* of the Christian redemption.

If you ask believers the reason why God sent His only begotten Son to the earth, most would respond, "So that when we die, we can go to Heaven."

That response above reflects our Platonic *linear* Greek thinking—not *circular/cyclical* Hebrew thinking. "Intellectually we are Greeks, not Hebrews" (Knowles 4). Plato's dualistic religious worldview overemphasized "spiritual world goals" that unduly influenced and corrupted God's *goals* of our restored relationship with Him and our renewed rulership over the earth.

"Someone" twisted the road sign. "Someone" pitched us a curve ball. We've swung and we've missed.

Many of us have been thrown off course by the reference in John 14:2 to the word "mansions" awaiting us in the Father's house:

*"In My Father's house are many mansions...**I go to prepare a place for you"*** (John 14:2). (Emphasis added).

As I stated in my book "God's Got A Problem (On His Hands)", I am normally a strong supporter of the King James translation over that of other Bibles. This is probably one of the few exceptions to that preference. Jesus spoke of many "dwelling places" in His Father's house, and that He was going away to prepare a place for those who were privileged to know Him. To use the word "mansion" rather than "dwelling place" may have been quite accurate for the life and times of the 17th century translators. However, for a modern-day reader, something was lost in translation in a big way. One of the most common dictionary meanings of the word mansion is that of a "large, imposing residence." People often learn words and concepts through picture linking or association. Unfortunately, in this case, this linking picture almost entirely takes the reference out of its context.

If one reads the same John chapter 14 *in its entirety*, one will readily observe that the Lord Jesus was referring to the fact that He dwells in the Father, and that the Father dwells in Him.

*"Do you not believe **that I am in the Father**, and the Father in Me? The words that I speak to you I do not speak on My own*

*authority; but the Father **who dwells in Me** does the works"* (John 14:10). (Emphasis added.)

In turn, man is to become the "dwelling place" or "home" of both God the Father and the Son, just as the Father was the abiding place of the Son. Jesus explains that it is the intention of the Father and the Son to make ***Their home*** in those who love and obey the Son.

"At that day you will know that I am in my Father, and you in Me, and I in you" (John 14:20).

... *"If anyone loves me, he will keep My word; and My Father will love him, **and We will come to him and make Our home with him*** (John 14:23). (Emphasis added.)

In the verse below in the same chapter 14 of John, ***Jesus identifies the Father, not Heaven,*** as our goal. He indicates that no one obtains the Father but by going through the Son.

*Jesus said to him, "I am the way, the truth, and the life. No one comes **to the Father** except through Me"* (John 14:6). (Emphasis added.)

Heaven is not the final end of our journey, nor is there any verse that describes Heaven as God's ***ultimate*** goal for us in our redemption. It is a temporary way station ***until*** the Lord calls us back to obedient post-resurrection earthly service. We are human beings, not angels, and have been made to eventually be ***resurrected and reunited back*** with our earthly bodies so that we may rule and reign with Christ on the earth.

It is a full ***circular*** experience.

But now Christ is risen from the dead, and has become the firstfruits of those who have fallen asleep. For since by man *came death, **by Man also came the resurrection of the dead**. For as in Adam all die, **even so in Christ all shall be made alive**. But each one in his own order: Christ the firstfruits, **afterward those who are Christ's at His coming**. Then comes the end, when He delivers the kingdom to God the Father, **when He puts an end to all rule and all authority and power**. For He must reign till He has put all enemies under His feet. The last enemy that will be destroyed is death"* (1 Corinthians 15:20–26). (Emphasis added.)

*Now may the God of peace Himself sanctify you completely; and may your whole spirit, soul, **and body** be preserved blameless at the coming of our Lord Christ* (1 Thessalonians 5:23). (Emphasis added.)

*And have made us kings and priests to our God; **and we shall reign on the earth**"* (Revelation 5:10). (Emphasis added.)

So, I have a question, probably just like you do: If Heaven is not the goal of the Christian redemption, then what is? Or perhaps the question should be *Who is?*

While performing church services for Hispanic inmates on Sunday evenings, without exception, I would hand the inmates Spanish Bibles for the weekly service. I would ask them to open their Bibles to the following verse:

"I am the way, the truth, and the life. No one comes to the Father except through me" (John 14:6).

I would often attempt to trick the inmates by intentionally misquoting the verse by substituting the word "Father" with the word "Heaven", reading the verse quickly then waiting for a reaction. Everyone would be looking straight at the verse and nodding their heads in agreement while I was misquoting it. Eventually, after several minutes, a lone individual inmate in the group would raise a hesitant hand to contend that his version of the Bible did not say the word "Heaven" but rather contained the word "Father". The surprised remainder of the group would quickly reread the verse to discover that *their assumption* regarding the goal of the Christian salvation was indeed *not* a place, but rather a Person—Father God. You can only imagine their shock to learn that the verse does *not* say *"No one comes to **Heaven** except through Me."* Rather, it clearly states, *"No one comes to the **Father** except through Me."*

After our original parents fell to Satan's rebellion, we lost God Himself and thus, we lost our eternal life. (See John 17:3 below). *The Father's goal in sending His Son* as an atoning sacrifice for our sin was *to return mankind back to the Father's original blueprint* of enjoying an *intimate relationship* with Him through which we have eternal life. When we are reconciled back to God, we are *regaining* our lost relationship with Him much like prodigal children returning *full circle back* to our Father. *Our relationship with God is the very definition of eternal life.* As we begin to *experientially* know the Father as the only true God as well as His Son, Jesus Christ, whom He sent, we then in turn begin to experience *eternal life (knowing God relationally)* in the here and now.

Therefore, eternal life must be a Person and not a place. Have a look at the next verse.

And this is eternal life, that they may know You, the only true God, and Jesus Christ whom You have sent (John 17:3).

So, What Difference Does The End Goal Make?

Defining the goal of the Christian life as laid out by Jesus is absolutely essential. Without a correctly defined goal, we are collectively wasting God's time and ours. And time is something that we cannot get back.

On one occasion, an inmate asked me what difference would it make if the goal of the Christian life did so happen to be a Person as opposed to a place.

In good Rabbinic Hebrew fashion, I answered his question with another question as to whether *he* thought it would make any difference. The inmate contemplated for several moments before ultimately concluding that it would indeed make a monumental difference. I asked him how. He responded that if the goal of the Christian life were a person rather than a place, then he would have to personally account for how he conducted himself at the conclusion of his life to that "Person." In contrast, if the goal were merely a place, the entry into that place would only require a mental agreement with points of dogma or doctrinal stances—a very Greek and linear notion, indeed. No change of the individual would be required other than the newly formed mental agreement with certain theological assertions. The condition of the heart issue would remain unaddressed and the internal rebellion virtually undisturbed within that person.

"The heart is deceitful above all things. And desperately wicked; Who can know it? I, the Lord, search the heart, I test the mind. Even to give every man according to his ways, According to the fruit of his doings" (Jeremiah 17:9–10).

Rebellion is not location-focused. It is heart-focused. It can occur in spiritual or in material environments and is clearly alive and well on earth today, even among believers. Simply going to a different place, no matter how marvelous, does not address God's problem of *rebellion within us* here *on earth*. As stated earlier, a spiritual creature (Satan) began the rebellion against God in a spiritual place called Heaven (Isaiah 14, Ezekiel 28).

Allow me to reiterate that: **The rebellion against God began in Heaven!**

The heavenly location and nearness to the throne of God did not prevent Satan's rebellion. By that same logic, simply dying and transferring from earth to Heaven does not change what or who we are. I have not yet found a verse in the Bible that indicates that we will be changed in our nature and character upon our physical death alone. Therefore, after the death of an unchanged person, God's problem of rebellion would continue on unchecked **wherever** that individual is taken. We can conclude that simply going to Heaven would not fix the internally implanted problem of rebellion entrenched within us.

Is there a "fix" to this problem of rebellion against Father God?

The Solution

The solution to the **problem of rebellion** is found in the one, singular prayer that Jesus taught us, "The Lord's Prayer":

*"Thy kingdom come. **Thy will be done on earth** as it is in heaven"* (Matthew 6:10). (Emphasis added.)

Jesus was **on earth** when He taught us this one simple prayer, and everything necessary to overthrow Satan's kingdom is contained within it. Can you imagine the impact on our earthly environment if we simply began to make the Lord's Prayer our **moment-by-moment** experience? What would happen to the atmosphere around us if we actually began doing God's will in a present tense context two seconds at a time?

If Jesus did not come to the earth to take us to Heaven, then why did He come?

He who sins is of the devil, for the devil has sinned from the beginning. **For this purpose** *the Son of God was manifested,* **that He might destroy the works of the devil** (rebellion) (1 John 3:8). (Emphasis and key word added.)

Inasmuch then as the children have partaken of flesh and blood, He Himself likewise shared in the same, that through death He might destroy him who had the power of death, that is, the devil,... (Hebrew 2:14).

For Christ also suffered once for sins, the just for the unjust, **that He might bring us to God***...*(1 Peter 3:18). (Emphasis added.)

who Himself bore our sins in His own body on the tree, **that we***, having died to sin,* **might live for righteousness***-by whose stripes you were healed* (1 Peter 2:24). (Emphasis added.)

He came to earth to end the rebellion against His Father*!* The **goal** of the Christian salvation is **to end the rebellion** against God the Father, and victory comes **by the doing of His will in all our matters***.*

Therefore, we make it our aim, whether present or absent, to be well pleasing to Him (2 Corinthians 5:9).

Therefore, since Christ suffered for us in the flesh, arm yourselves also with the same mind, for he who has suffered in the flesh has ceased from sin, that he no longer should live the rest of his time in the flesh for the lusts of men, **but for the will of God** (1 Peter 4:1–2). (Emphasis added.)

*And having been perfected, He became the author of eternal salvation **to all who obey Him*** (Hebrews 5:9). (Emphasis added.)

"If you love Me, keep My commandments" (John 14:15).

Jesus said to them, *"My food **is to do the will of Him** who sent Me, and to finish His work"* (John 4:34). (Emphasis added.)

Satan's rebellion in the form of "the works of the devil" is all around us. The rebellion of independence from God is still in us and is causing chaos, frenzy, turmoil, confusion, disease, death and destruction on our earth. Just read the headlines of any newspaper or on the Internet or watch any local news channel. Satan would love nothing more than for all the saints to leave behind their buried human bodies and ascend to the spirit world as disembodied spirits permanently abandoning the earth for the spiritual Heaven, never to return to earth, leaving him completely in charge.

We have been sold a Greek/Platonic linear bill of goods!

Jesus came so that **He might destroy the works of the devil.** Our returning King, Jesus Christ of Nazareth and we, **the overcoming** saints, will eventually judge and destroy all of Satan's works, whether those works are on our earth or in the second Heaven.

*Do you not know that the **saints will judge** the world? ... Do you not know that **we shall judge angels**? How much more, things that pertain to this life?* (1 Corinthians 6: 2–3). (Emphasis added.)

Now I saw heaven opened, and behold, a white horse. And He who sat on him was called Faithful and True, and in righteousness He judges and makes war. His eyes were like a flame of fire and on His head were many crowns. He had a name written that no one knew except Himself. He was clothed with a robe dipped in blood, and His name is called the Word of God. **And the armies in heaven clothed in fine linen, white and clean, followed Him on white horses.** *Now out of His mouth comes a sharp sword, that with it He should strike the nations. And He Himself will rule them with a rod of iron. He Himself treads the winepress of the fierceness and wrath of Almighty God. And He has on His robe and on His thigh a name written:* KING OF KINGS AND LORD OF LORDS (Revelation 19:11–16). (Emphasis added.)

*"**And they overcame him** by the blood of the Lamb and by the word of their testimony, and they did not love their lives to the death* (Revelation 12:11). (Emphasis added.)

And I saw thrones, and they sat on them, **and judgment was committed to them.** *Then I saw the souls of those who had been beheaded for their witness to Jesus and for the word of God, who had not worshiped the beast or his image, and had not received his mark on their foreheads or on their hands. And they lived and reigned with Christ for a thousand years* (Revelation 20:4). (Emphasis added.)

However, **judgment** must begin in the house of God **first.**

For the time has come for judgment to begin at the house of God; and if it begins with us first, what will be the end of those who do not obey the gospel of God? (1 Peter 4:17).

Taking us to Heaven **by itself** does not fix anything. **Ending the rebellion inside of us** and on earth **changes everything.** As the inmates in the jail put into daily practice **the solution,** ("Thy will be done"), to the ongoing problem of rebellion against God, things completely changed within that dark jail.

God intends to change the rebellious atmosphere on earth by bringing His Kingdom directly to it.

*"Behold, the Lord comes **with ten thousands of His saints**, to execute judgment on all, to convict all who are ungodly among them of all their ungodly deeds which they have committed in an ungodly way, and of all the harsh things which ungodly sinners have spoken against Him"*(Jude 14–15). (Emphasis added).

The struggle involves spiritual warfare of kingdom versus kingdom and no doubt the existing government of spiritual rebellion will resist its impending replacement with all its might. Yet we the saints *will return to earth in a military maneuver* with Jesus Christ as the returning King. Jesus will displace the usurper who stole *our earthly inheritance*, and we will take back that which rightfully *belongs to us*—the *earthly* kingdom that was originally granted to us in God's original blueprint.

The Gospel of the Kingdom is about the soon-*coming* Kingdom, *not* the soon-*escaping* Church. The Father's plan to reestablish the Kingdom of God over the fallen earth involves *restoring our relationship* with Him along with *restoring* our *responsibility to rule* the earth and its nations. His perfect plan involved sending His Son Jesus Christ as the atoning sacrifice to assuage the Father's ire caused by our rebellion. Jesus' obedience to God built a bridge of blood for us to be able to cross back over *to return* to our Father.

Again, we see God completing His *full circle blueprint.*

In Summary

The Middle Eastern, Hebrew perspective of a *circular/ cyclical* world differs dramatically from the Greek *linear* viewpoint of

Western thinking. The Hebrew, on one hand, defines his world and his time in terms of *cyclical patterns* and historical events that reflect the self-evident presence and significance of repetitive *cycles* in God's created nature. On the other hand, Greek thinking leads to frustration with present-moment time and to systematic *linear* explanations of the universe and of God. Greek Platonic thinking and corresponding Gnosticism lead away from an "inferior" time-constrained earth to a "superior timeless celestial" goal.

Nevertheless, the Hebrew still understands that the Father declared on the 6th day that His entire creation, including the earth, mankind and the animal kingdom was *"very good."* The Hebrew also knows that God never changed His mind as to that opinion despite mankind's fall into spiritual rebellion. Jews experientially understand that God is a God of "Aliyah" who *redeems and restores in cycles and circles*.

The entire history of the nation and people of Israel is a testimony to this Creator God of *circular* second chances.

The Bible story is one of a *circular/cyclical restorative* blueprint.

God's Army has been thrown off of God's targeted objective of *restoration* of relationship and earthly rulership. As a result, the insidious encroachment of Greek, Platonic *linear* thinking has perverted Hebrew, *circular/cyclical* experiences of "aliyah" return. God's target is for His people *to come back* to Him and *to come back* home to their earth. The Hebrew notion of *salvation* involves *deliverance* from the hands of one's enemies and *circular redemption back* to God and *back* to one's bequeathed land.

Going to Heaven *as our permanent home* puts us on a Greek, Platonic, *linear* trajectory, *away* from Earth, *away* from God's originally designed blueprint found in Genesis chapter 1:26–31. *Returning* to God our Father and to the earth as our permanent home puts us on a Hebrew *circular* trajectory, *back towards* God's original blueprint.

I have yet to find a verse in the Holy Scripture that identifies Heaven as our *permanent* home. A *circular* study of the Hebrew Scripture (*both* Old and New Testaments) does *not* take us to Heaven as our *permanent* domicile. Heaven seems to be a way station until our disembodied spirits are reunited with our resurrected and glorified bodies at the Lord's second coming to earth. Meanwhile, we begin to prepare to take back our original God-given inheritance (the earth), *as designed in His original blueprint*. We are coming *back home* to our Father *and* to our bequeathed *inheritance, the earth*. Our permanent dwelling places of rest include Father God, Jesus and our earth (Isaiah 66:1–2; John 14–17).

Our *circular return* to our destiny of rulership over the earth can be seen in Revelation chapter 20:6 where it describes the overcoming saints as being blessed and holy because they are able to participate in the first resurrection now that the second death has no power over them. It immediately follows with the proclamation that these same overcoming saints shall be priests of God and shall reign with Him 1000 years. Revelation 5:10 states we have been made kings and priests to our God and we shall reign *on the earth*. We will have come back home—a full circle!

The Bible does not speak much about what we will do in Heaven after we pass away and are *temporarily* separated from our earthly bodies.

However, the Bible *does speak a great deal* about *what* we will be doing *and where* we will be doing it *after* our bodily resurrections. Most of the future action and battles discussed in the Bible concerning the restoration of God's Kingdom and the replacement of Satan's kingdom over the earth *take place— right here on the earth*.

The earth and its nations (kingdoms) were the very stakes that Jesus and Satan were focusing on in the second temptation of Christ in Luke 4:5–8. They understood that the end game involves the jurisdiction of rulership over the earth and its kingdoms. (See Psalms 2:8.)

Heaven, *including* the presence of God and the Heavenly city, the New Jerusalem, *finally returns back* to earth, a *circular restoration* to the Father's perfect blueprint. Chapters 21 and 22 of the *final* book of the Bible, Revelation, describe the converging *full circle returns* of Heaven *back* to the earth along with *restoration of relationship* between God and man. It describes the overcoming saints' reward of earthly rule under the headship of Christ.

It is a *full circle* experience and a *full circle ending* to the greatest story.

The Bible must be taught *in a circle*, not a straight line.

Chapter 3

Relationship: You're Family

Our Heavenly Father deeply loves us and yearns to have a relationship of rest with us. If anyone doubts that, all they have to do is look at the cross of Jesus of Nazareth, "Yeshua" (Hebrew meaning: "God's salvation") (Biltz 23), to know that there's no deeper love than for God to send His only begotten Son to the earth as an atonement sacrifice canceling out our death-producing rebellion. The anger of the Father against our rebellion needed to be assuaged. Christ's **obedient** sacrifice resulted in building a bridge of blood to once again provide us access **back** to our Father.

For Christ also suffered once for sins, the just for the unjust, ***that He might bring us to God***...*(1 Peter 3:18a).* (Emphasis added.)

A couple of the most descriptive verses revealing that it is the Father's desire to have a **relationship of rest** with His children are found in Isaiah 66:1–2:

Thus says the Lord: "Heaven is My throne, and earth is My footstool, ***Where is the house that you will build for Me? And where is the place of My rest?*** *For all those things My hand has made, and all those things exist, "Says the Lord. '**But on this one** will I look: On him who is poor and of a contrite spirit, And who trembles at my word"* (Isaiah 66:1–2). (Emphasis added.)

Man, by design, is hard-wired for relationship with God. Prior to truly **knowing** Jesus and the Father, people often refer to a large empty hole within them that they are continually trying to fill with various things—often to no avail. This is because the ingredients they are using in an attempt to fill the void were never designed to fit the contours of their empty space. The bogus promises of happiness that the world's value system offers us usually result in frustration, emptiness, futility and depression. Yet, we stubbornly continue to explore spurious offers of satisfaction, not appreciating that our true permanent joy only comes from emotionally *knowing* God and having a relationship with the One who formed us from the very beginning.

*For **You formed my inward parts**; You covered me in my mother's womb. I will praise You, **for I am fearfully and wonderfully made**; marvelous are Your works, and that my soul knows very well. My frame was not hidden from You, when I was made in secret, **and skillfully wrought** in the lowest parts of the earth. Your eyes saw my substance, being yet unformed... How precious also are Your thoughts to me O God! How great is the sum of them! If I should count them, they would be more in number than the sand; **when I awake I am still with You*** (Psalm 139:13–18). (Emphasis added.)

What does this love relationship of rest look like?

Love is sticking your neck out for others. Love is sacrificing yourself for others. Love is obeying God to please Him (Clampett 3). Characteristics of love include loyalty, self-sacrifice, time investment, emotional commitment and desire to please.

Therefore we make it our aim, whether present or absent, to be well pleasing to Him (2 Corinthians 5:9).

Why does Jesus in the verses cited below emphasize the *crucial importance* of our having a relationship with our Divine Father?

*"For God so loved the world that He gave His only begotten Son, that whoever believes in Him should not perish **but have everlasting life** (John 3:16). (Emphasis added.)*

*"And **this is eternal life**, that **they may know You**, the only true God, and Jesus Christ whom You have sent (John 17:3). (Emphasis added.)*

As these verses describe, eternal life is not so much a condition as it is a relationship. ***Eternal life is a personal relationship*** with a Divine Person, namely Our Heavenly Father. Eternal life is not so much a "what" but rather is a "Who". Thus, ***without a personal relationship*** with that Divine "Who", we are simply dead men walking without Life. You see, even though our hearts physically beat in our chests and we have brain waves that can be monitored on a screen, God sees us as already dead when we are separated from Him. The only way we can come alive in the Father's eyes is to return to Him by forming a relationship first with His son, Jesus Christ of Nazareth, whose job it is to reintroduce us back to our Father.

Jesus said to him, *"I am the way, the truth, **and the life**. No one comes **to the Father** except through Me"* (John 14:6). (Emphasis added.)

God the Father initially had a vibrant relationship with Adam based on trust. He delegated to Adam awesome responsibilities.

Then the Lord God took the man and put him in the garden of Eden to tend and keep it (Genesis 2:15).

Out of the ground the Lord formed every beast of the field and every bird of the air, and brought them to Adam to see what he would call them. And whatever Adam called each living creature, that was its name (Genesis 2:19).

However, that relationship with God was lost in the fall of man in the garden. Adam and Eve were separated from the presence of God and removed from the earthly Garden of Paradise due to their acceptance and affiliation with the spiritual rebellion against the laws of God. Adam, as the first man, squandered what was freely given to him because he did not appreciate the value of what he possessed. (Sound familiar?) He already had eternal life because he had a relationship with God. When that relationship with God was broken through Adam and Eve's buying into Satan's rebellion against God's laws, they lost their relationship with God, causing them to be separated from the Father. Their physical separation from God when removed from the garden also produced emotional and spiritual separation. *Their complete separation from the Father resulted* in their spiritual and eventual physical death. Consequently, because of the impact of generational curses, we also suffer death. Without relationship with God, we are separated from Him, making us nothing more than dead men walking.

God's goal is to restore His relationship with mankind, first through His Son Yeshua (Jesus of Nazareth) then later with Him as our Father, which brings about eternal life both individually and corporately.

Our *corporate* restoration of relationship experience is mentioned in Revelation chapters 21 and 22. These chapters reveal that God the Father *will again dwell* with His people who belong to Him in a *renewed intimate relationship*—much like the heavenly city New Jerusalem coming down out of Heaven back to the new earth prepared as a bride adorned for her husband. Just as the tribes of Israel camped around the presence of God during the wilderness wanderings on their journey from Egypt towards Canaan, the tabernacle of God will likewise be in our midst as He wipes away every tear from our eyes, removing death, sorrow and crying. The accompanying promise is that we who overcome shall inherit all things, and God shall be our God, and we shall be His children (relationship restored).

Then I, John, saw the holy city, New Jerusalem, coming down out of heaven from God, prepared as a bride adorned for her husband. And I heard a loud voice from heaven saying, "Behold, the tabernacle of God is with men, **and He will dwell with them, and they shall be His people.** *God Himself will be with them and be their God. And God will wipe away every tear from their eyes; there shall be no more death, nor sorrow, nor crying. There shall be no more pain, for the former things have passed away"* (Revelation 21:2–4). (Emphasis added.) (Relationship restored.)

Our ***personal*** restoration of relationship begins in Revelation 3:20-21 with Jesus standing at the door of the individual person and knocking. If any one hears His voice and opens the door, Jesus will come into him and dine with him with the promise that he who overcomes will be granted to sit with Jesus on His throne, just as Jesus overcame and sat down with His Father on His throne.

"To him who overcomes I will grant to sit with Me on **My throne,** *as I also overcame and sat down with My Father* **on His throne"** (Revelation 3:21). (Emphasis added.)

"He who overcomes shall inherit all things, **and I will be his God and he shall be My Son"** (Revelation 21:7). (Emphasis added.) (Relationship restored.)

We're God's Family!

In the process of forming a lasting relationship, fathers typically give their children three things:

1. Identity
2. Protection
3. Provision

As to our *divine identity*, we need to ask ourselves the following:

How does God the Father see us?

Are we not to identify ourselves as He sees us?

Our Heavenly Father as our Father desires to impart to us the extraordinary reality that we are children and heirs of the most high God. As such, we are to appropriate (claim ownership) of our new divine identity.

Recently, when teaching a Bible study to a church group, I was presenting a teaching referring to the fact that we are to accept our bequeathed identity as adopted children of God's family.

*For you did not receive the spirit of bondage again to fear, but you received the **Spirit of adoption** by whom we cry out, "Abba, Father." The Spirit Himself bears witness with our spirit **that we are children of God**, and if children, then heirs— **heirs of God and joint heirs with Christ**, if indeed we suffer with Him, that we may also be glorified together* (Romans 8:15–17). (Emphasis added.)

When considering your identity in God's family, ponder the beginning words of the Lord's Prayer.

*"In this manner, therefore pray: **Our Father** in heaven, Hallowed be Your name..."* (Matthew 6:9). (Emphasis added.)

I opened the teaching by introducing what I thought to be the most significant word in the entire Bible: **"Our"**. The word is found in the strategic location as the very first word of the Lord's Prayer. During the class, the Holy Spirit inspired me to emphasize that the first word **"our"** in the Lord's Prayer *actually reveals* our family identity of relationship with the Godhead and with one another.

I asked the group what impact it had on them once they realized that it was Jesus who was instructing us on how to pray to "our" Father, and that it was Jesus who taught us how to begin the prayer with the personal pronoun *"our"*. As they took a moment to contemplate the significance of the question, I could see the light bulbs coming on. They were beginning to become aware that when Jesus Christ was teaching "The Lord's Prayer", He was speaking to us, the listeners, as members of the same family who happen to *possess the same Father.*

I then asked the class that since it was Jesus who taught us how we were mutually to pray "The Lord's Prayer" to "our" Father, what did that make Jesus to them in the family sense? Logically, my students figured out that the Jesus must be *their older brother* since He used the collective pronoun "our" to define our mutual relationship with "our" Father. The students suddenly realized that they belonged to God as genuine members of His divine family! Jesus as our older brother points the way to *our* mutual Father, thus making us part of the same divine family.

"I am the way the truth, and the life. No one comes to the Father except through me" (John 14:6).

*"In this manner, therefore, pray: **Our Father** in heaven, Hallowed be Your name* (Matthew 6:9). (Emphasis added.)

Study the word **"our"**. I contend that it is the most awesome word in the Bible. It applies to all the saints. All sincere disciples of Christ are eligible. The word "our" in "The Lord's prayer" provides us with an essential and unique gift—the most important gift for which all mankind yearns. It is the realization that we intrinsically **belong** to the most important unit ever established: **the divine family of God.** When we realize the truth about our divine family membership, it produces in us is the indispensable appreciation that we have taken on **a new identity** as "our Father's" precious children. This fact connects us to our Divine Father first vertically and later to our brothers and sisters in the Lord horizontally. We need **to emotionally and intellectually own** this new identity as children of our loving, divine Father.

Ownership of how we identify ourselves in God changes everything!

It answers the question, *To **Whom** do we belong?*

*But when the fullness of the time had come, God sent forth His Son, born of a woman, born under the law, to redeem those who were under the law, **that we might receive the adoption as sons**. And **because you are sons**, God has sent forth the Spirit of His Son into your hearts crying out **"Abba, Father!"** Therefore you are no longer a slave **but a son, and if a son, then an heir of God through Christ*** (Galatians 4:4–7).

And you are Christ's and Christ is God's (1 Corinthians 3:23).

It also answers the question, ***What** is the Father constructing in us?*

When we begin to own our divine identity, the empty hole within us begins to become filled. We become complete by inviting God into our private lives not only to visit, but also to remain and stay.

"If anyone loves Me, he will keep My word; **and My Father** *will love him,* **and We will come to him and make Our home with Him** (John 14:23). (Emphasis added.)

We become free of the bondage and torment of trying to live our lives in a distant manner from God. We become full of hope and expectation. Our lives become exciting and challenging in a completely unique way. Life begins to make sense and take on a significant purpose.

Lastly, it answers the question, *What inures to our benefit, if anything, in our new roles as family members (children) of the Most High God?*

As children and divine family members of "Our Father", we will receive an inheritance *of all things*, including the earth and its nations, **as heirs and coheirs with Christ if indeed** we suffer with Him so that we may also be glorified together (Romans 8:17).

I will declare the decree: The Lord has said to Me, You are my Son, Today I have begotten You. Ask of Me, and I will give You **the nations** *for* **Your inheritance,** *And the* **ends of the earth** *for Your possession* (Psalms 2:7–8). (Emphasis added.) (Inheritance as co-heirs with Christ.)

"He who overcomes shall inherit all things, **and I will be his God and he shall be My son** (Revelation 21:7). (Relationship resulting in inheritance.)

What a thought! It is difficult at first to wrap our minds around these truths. Nevertheless, this is God's norm. It is His blueprint plan for us. We are the ones who have to change our perceptions.

Besides identity, what else do fathers provide to their children? **Protection**.

Have a look at the following verses:

For the Lord's portion is His people; Jacob is the place of His inheritance. "He found him in a desert land and in the wasteland, a howling wilderness; **He encircled him***, He instructed him,* **He kept him** *as the apple of His eye. As an eagle stirs up its nest***, hovers over its young, spreading out its wings***, taking them up***, carrying them on its wings***, so the Lord alone led him...* (Deuteronomy 32:9–12). (Emphasis added.)

The eternal God **is your refuge***, and* **underneath are the everlasting arms** (Deuteronomy 33:27). (Emphasis added.)

The Lord also will be a refuge for the oppressed, A refuge in times of trouble. And those who know Your name will put their trust in You; **for You, Lord, have not forsaken those who seek You** (Psalm 9: 9–10). (Emphasis added.)

God is our refuge *and strength,* **a very present help in trouble***. Therefore we will not fear, even though the earth be removed...*(Psalm 46:1–2). (Emphasis added.)

What else do fathers give to their children?

Provision.

Jesus in Luke chapter 12 was attempting to explain to His disciples and to the multitude that life is more than temporary food. He invites the listeners to observe all around them that it is *Father God* who feeds the birds that do not work. It is *Father God* who clothes the flowers that do not spin or toil. He then declares *that the Father is fully aware* that we need food and clothing. Jesus prioritizes that we should first seek the Kingdom of God and as a result of our proper alignment of priorities, all of our temporal needs will be added to us.

Jesus wraps up this topic with the assurance that we have nothing to fear because it is our Father's good pleasure to give us the Kingdom.

"Do not fear, little flock, for it is your Father's good pleasure to give you the kingdom (Luke 12:32).

Paul the Apostle ended his letter to the Philippians with the following declaration based on his personal experience:

*And my God **shall supply all your need** according to His riches in glory by Christ Jesus. Now to our God **and Father** be glory forever and ever. Amen.* (Philippians 4:19–20) (Emphasis added.)

Now that we understand that our identity is that of members of God's family and that our Father will protect and provide for us, wouldn't it be prudent to understand what the Head of our family deems to be *His* essential goals for us?

God's 4 Goals of Relationship

The overarching **goal** of the Father is to be **reconnected with His people** by means of a **renewed relationship**.

Relationship with our Father comes about as we are made into a **dwelling place** for Him. As the Godhead begins to dwell within us, we come into **union** with both the Son (Yeshua) and our Father. Our newly formed union produces the formation of God's *image* within us reaching out to the world. Union with the Father and the Son ultimately brings about *our rest* in God and *His rest* in us. These goals are similar yet even more profound than what Adam and Eve experienced before the fall. The 4 goals of renewed relationship are:

1. To become His *Dwelling Place*
2. To be in *union* with Him
3. To be brought into His *image*
4. To enter into His *rest*

To begin with, our *relationship* with our Father begins anew to be *reconnected* as we children of God *respond* to a *personal* invitation extended to us *from* God's Son, Jesus Christ.

*"Behold I stand at the door and knock. If anyone hears My voice and opens the door, **I will come in to him** and dine with him, and he with Me"* (Revelation 3:20). (Emphasis added.)

The first goal is reflected in Yeshua (Jesus of Nazareth) initiating contact by standing at the door of our heart and knocking. He will not kick down the door. If there is to be a relationship, its nature must be one of free will on the part of both parties.

As we hear Yeshua's voice, we have to make a decision whether to open the door to our interior (heart, mind, soul and spirit) and invite Him in. As we respond to Christ's overtures of love, it is impossible to remain the same.

As in Revelation 3:20 listed above, we normally dine with intimate friends or family. As we learn to receive the divine love Jesus imparts to us, we are introduced to the concept that Jesus is the beginning of a larger, nascent relationship with

70

"our Father". Our older brother Jesus of Nazareth desires to complete His delegated task of reacquainting us with our mutual Father.

"I am the way, the truth, and the life. No one comes to the Father except through Me (John 14:6).

As we invite the Son to enter into our interior so that we may dine together, the ultimate point of the dinner date is to eventually invite a Second Guest.

*Jesus answered and said to him," If anyone loves Me, he will keep My word; and My Father will love him, **and We will come to him and make Our home with him*** (John 14:23).

A dinner invitation is for special guests and relatives. It is designed for eventual intimacy.

If, as John 14:21 suggests, the ultimate goal of the Father and Son is to make Their home with us and in us, then we in essence will have become a *dwelling place* for our God. It answers the question God asks in Isaiah 66:1–2:

*Thus says the Lord: "Heaven is My throne, and earth is My footstool. **Where is the house that you will build for me? And where is the place of My rest?** For all those things my hand has made, and all those things exist," Says the Lord. **But on this one will I look**: on him who is poor and of a contrite spirit and who trembles at My word* (Isaiah 66:1–2). (Emphasis added.)

Even after the fall of mankind to Satan's rebellion, our Father continued to have a yearning for **union** with His children. God will not be at rest until we invite Him to move into our human houses in which He desires to dwell. Scripture explains to us that we are God's houses, and He is ours.

As we allow the Father and the Son to remain in us to dine in Their dwelling place, something eternally special begins to develop. We begin to form the second goal of **union** with the Divine Godhead.

*"that they all may be one, **as you, Father, are in me, and I in You; that they also may be one in Us, that the world may believe that You sent Me**. I in them, and You in Me; that they may be made perfect in one, and that the world may know that you have sent Me, and have loved them as You have loved Me"* (John 17:21,23). (Emphasis added.)

The **purpose** of God **reconnecting relationally** with His children by means of becoming one with them through **union** is **so that the world may believe** that the Father sent His Son as we see in verse 21 of John chapter 17 cited in the paragraph above.

Additionally, as this **relationship of union** forms between the Father **with us** as His children, we begin to change. This change that we begin to experience is profound, unique and brings us into God's third goal: our beginning to actually change into God's **image**.

*Then God said, "**Let us make man in Our image**, according to Our likeness;..."* (Genesis 1:26) (Emphasis added.)

*But we all, with unveiled face, beholding as in a mirror the glory of the Lord, are being transformed **into the same image** from glory to glory, just as by the Spirit of the Lord* (2 Corinthians 3:18). (Emphasis added).

This goal **fulfills** God's original blueprint. We were created initially in God's image, and through the blood of Christ, we are to reflect His image to those who do not know Him. Once again, this phenomenon describes a **circular** fulfillment experience. The result: our image being transformed in the here and now.

I beseech you therefore, brethren, by the mercies of God, that you present your bodies a living sacrifice, holy, acceptable to God, which is your reasonable service. ***And do not to be conformed to this world, but be transformed by the renewing of your mind, that you may prove what is that good and acceptable and perfect will of God*** (Romans 12:1–2). (Emphasis added.)

As we begin ***to carry out*** the Father's perfect will ***in every dimension*** of our lives, we begin to reflect more and more of ***the image of Christ*** for the benefit of the world that does not yet know God.

"I in them, and You in Me; that they may be made perfect in one, ***and that the world may know that You have sent Me,*** *and have loved them as you have loved me* (John 17:23). (Emphasis added.)

We see ***the original blueprint circular restoration*** producing God's 4th goal to ultimately be ***at rest*** with His people. As we invite Him to enter His human dwelling place, the Father is finally at ***rest***.

I have a theory: I see Father God ***finally at rest only*** when He has actually been invited into to a human house that has been built exclusively for Him.

The verse cited in the beginning of this chapter reflects the ultimate goal of our Divine Father. It bears repeating:

This says the Lord: "Heaven is My throne, and earth is my footstool. ***Where is the house that you will build for Me? And where is the place of My rest?*** *For all those things My hand* *has made, and all those things exist," says the Lord. "But **on this one will I look**: on him who is poor and of a contrite spirit, and who trembles at My Word* (Isaiah 66:1–2).

The title of this book is "The Blueprint". Our Father is a builder. Our older Brother is a carpenter. They are in the process of building an everlasting structure. This structure is one that *reflects* the light of God, eternal life, and boundless joy. This structure reflects these things because of what (or better said, Who) dwells inside.

*Now, therefore, you are no longer strangers and foreigners, but fellow citizens with the saints and **members of the household of God**, having been **built** on the **foundation** of the apostles and prophets, Jesus Christ Himself being the **chief cornerstone**, in whom the **whole building being fitted together, grows into a holy temple in the Lord, in whom you also are being built together for a dwelling place of God in the Spirit*** (Ephesians 2:19-22). (Emphasis added.)

Union with God by *indwelling His children at long last* produces *rest* between God and man.

But what does that *rest* look like?

Renewed *relationship* with God that produces rest simply means we can be ourselves and begin to spend time with our loving Father. We can put our ear on His chest and listen to His heartbeat. We can climb up onto His lap and look up into His eyes, sharing with Him all our emotions, questions, "hang-ups" and confusions. We just learn to relax and spend time like a *sponge* soaking up His love while in His embrace.

On one occasion, the Father specifically instructed me to act like a sponge. I asked the Father whether acting so would bring on passivity. He answered my question with another question, asking me what the purpose of a sponge is. I responded that it was to float in its water environment while absorbing and soaking in its surroundings. His next question dealt with what happens to a sponge when it becomes saturated. I answered that the abundance of water in the form of runoff would go out and away from the sponge.

What I heard back from Him was the verse in John chapter 7 when Jesus declared on the last day of the Feast of Tabernacles, *"If anyone thirsts, let him come to Me and drink. He who believes in Me, as the Scripture has said, **out of his heart will flow rivers of living water"** (John 7:37–38). (Emphasis added.)

I then understood that as a sponge I would be able to float *at rest* in the liquid environment of the love of the Father, soaking in all that could be absorbed until I reached a saturation point. The *"at rest"* absorption of living water, the very presence of God was to be my task as His son. The absorption was to take place as a *natural* result of our Father-son relationship becoming more intimate. The intimacy would include spending more time together, speaking more with one another and just enjoying one another's presence. I was now part of the divine family. Intimacy with Him was not to be a task of striving, but rather one of *rest* by entering the rest of God. As I soaked up the living water of God, I discovered that the overflow was not for me. It was designed to be the source of life for the benefit of other needy people.

For he who has entered His rest has himself also ceased from his works as God did from His. Let us therefore be diligent to enter that rest, lest anyone fall according to the same example of disobedience (Hebrews 4:10–11).

Part of the role of being a *child* of God and pursuing a more intimate *relationship* with our Father, is learning how to function within God's order of His Kingdom.

"He who has my commandments and keeps them, it is he who loves Me. And he who loves Me will be loved by My Father, and I will love him and manifest Myself to him" (John 14:21). (Emphasis added.)

Kingdom in this context does not refer so much to a place but rather to His **government**. It is not so much an issue of the King's domain as it is the King's dominion. *"Your kingdom come, **Your will be done on earth** as it is in heaven"*(Matthew 6:10). (Emphasis added.)

Effectively carrying out God's will in particular problematic situations requires us to "go vertical" in order *to inquire* of the Father as to what He desires relative to our actions and words in the particular moment. All we have to do is ask. We do not have to figure things out on our own. We are to be *at rest* with God while awaiting His guidance, instructions, and direction through the Holy Spirit as to *what* to do, *what* to say and *when/where* to do and say it.

The "go vertical" approach involves the opening of a conversation in dialogue form with God the Father, much in the same way we would with our human fathers. Whenever we dialogue with our Father, our relationship intensifies and becomes more intimate. We ask Him questions; He provides us answers. We begin to simply know Him better. We start to become one with Him as we see in the Gospel of John chapters 14 and 17. Based on our Father quietly providing us instruction and direction as to how to best carry out His will in a particular circumstance, we are finally *at rest* in Him, as He is in us. *As we learn to obey to carry out His will* in all our matters, we in turn begin to experience what *God's rest* looks and feels like.

When we ask the Father in the Lord's Prayer to send His Kingdom and to have His will be done in our lives on earth, we begin to experience the Father's divine order. When the Father's divine order is brought to bear on our challenging situations or circumstances, we sense improvement with the resulting fruit of the Spirit of Peace. Often God's peace is immediately tangible and notable. We come into a sense of being *at rest* with God. When *we simply do His will* in the midst of our challenges and circumstances, *we are at rest* and *God is at rest.*

And to whom did He swear that they would not enter His rest, but to those who did not obey? (Hebrews 3:18).

For he who has entered His rest has himself also ceased from his works as God did from His (Hebrews 4:10).

There are seven feasts of the Lord that are celebrated by the nation of Israel. The culmination of the seven Hebrew feasts occurs during the month of *Tishri*, which is the seventh month of the ecclesiastical year. The seventh feast is called Sukkot, which is also known as the Feast of Tabernacles or Feast of Booths. It is represented by the building of booths in which the Jews would *dwell* for seven days. The Jews *dwelling in the booths* during the last feast, the Feast of Tabernacles, is a *representation* of our dwelling in God, and God in turn dwelling in us. It demonstrates the end of the line of our maturity, finally acquiring *God's rest by dwelling* in His presence and allowing His presence to dwell in us.

*And they found written in the law which the Lord had commanded by Moses that the children **of Israel should dwell in booths** during the feast of the seventh month, and that they should announce and proclaim and all their cities and in Jerusalem, saying, "Go out to the mountain, and bring olive branches, branches of oil trees, myrtle branches, palm* *branches, and branches of leafy trees, **to make booths**, as it is written." Then the people went out and brought them and **made themselves booths**, each one on the roof of his house, or in their courtyards or the courts of the house of God...So the whole assembly of those who had returned from the captivity **made booths and sat under the booths**; for since the days of Joshua the son of Nun until that day the children of Israel had not done so. And there was very great gladness* (Nehemiah 8:14–17). (Emphasis added.)

"If anyone loves Me, he will keep My word; *and My Father will love him, and We will come to him **and make Our home** with him."* (John 14:23). (Emphasis added.)

*Or do you not know that **your body is the temple of the Holy Spirit** who is in you, whom you have from God, and you are not your own? For you were bought at a price; therefore glorify God in your body and in your spirit which are God's.* (1 Corinthians 6:19–20) (Emphasis added.)

*but Christ as a Son over His own house, **whose house we are** if we hold fast the confidence and the rejoicing of the hope firm to the end* (Hebrews 3:6). (Emphasis added.)

*And I heard a loud voice from heaven saying, "**Behold the tabernacle of God** is with men **and He will dwell with them**, and they shall be His people. God Himself will be with them and be their God"* (Revelation 21:3). (Emphasis added.)

Dwelling with God brings rest to us. Our allowing God to dwell inside of us **in obedience** to Him also **brings rest** to Him. **Dwelling with God reflects a restoration of our relationship together.**

God's blueprint plan for **relationship** is **restored**, and we will have come *full circle*.

We will have returned *back to the beginning*—this time, for eternity.

Chapter Four

Rulership: You're Royalty

The study of God's blueprint and the Gospel of the Kingdom *reveal God's goals* for mankind, which in turn leads to the next topic of the *roles* He has designed for us.

We have already discussed how a relationship of trust existed between God and Adam prior to his fall. This relationship prompted a transfer of privileges and responsibilities of stewarding over the earthly creation from God the Father to man (Genesis 1 and 2). We also discussed that our relationship with God reveals *our membership status* in His divine family, including the benefits and responsibilities of our inheritance.

We are children of God and as His children, we are also God's heirs *as well as joint heirs* with Christ if we suffer with Him (Romans 8:16-17). (See also Galatians 3:29-4:1-7).

Webster's Dictionary definition of "heir" is "one who inherits or is entitled to inherit property, a hereditary rank, title or office" (*Merriam-Webster.com*, Merriam-Webster, 2015. Web. 10 July 2015). The word "inheritance" is defined as "property, money, and traits of character or features that descend to an heir, typically from parent to child" (*Merriam-Webster.com*, Merriam-Webster, 2015. Web. 10 July 2015). A synonym of heritage includes the word "birthright", which applies to property, rank or privilege coming by right of birth.

Now that we see our familial connection to the Godhead, it is critical to understand that based on that connection, He desires to give us the earthly kingdom as our inheritance. God's creation on earth was to be subdued and cared for by our first parents and their offspring. Nations of people would begin to appear as man carried out the mandate to fill the earth by being fruitful and multiplying. The earth was always ours to begin with, but we unfortunately squandered our inheritance. Nevertheless, we will help take it back as obedient children of Father God and as co-heirs with His Son Jesus Christ.

*But seek the kingdom of God, and all these things shall be added to you. Do not fear, little flock, **for it is your Father's good pleasure to give you the kingdom** (Luke 12:31–32). (Emphasis added.)*

*I will declare the decree: the Lord has said to Me, You are my Son, today I have begotten You. Ask of Me, and I will give You the **nations for Your inheritance, and the ends of the earth for Your possession** (Psalms 2: 7–8). (Emphasis added.)*

If Jesus' inheritance consists of the nations and the ends of the earth, then as co-heirs with Christ, we *also* shall receive the *same* inheritance. (See Romans 8:15-17.)

Ponder that for a moment, wrapping your heart and mind around that truth!

We earlier saw Satan's temptation of Jesus by showing Him all the kingdoms of the world in Luke chapter 4. Satan promised to give it all to Christ if He would only bow down before Satan and worship him. Jesus dispatched Satan with the admonition that only the Lord God is to be worshiped and served. Ever since this encounter, the two kingdoms of light and darkness have remained locked in mortal combat over the two ultimate prizes: the earth and all the nations that inhabit it, ***both of which were part of God's original blueprint.***

God cares deeply about the nations and their people to whom He desires to manifest Himself through His agents. We in the

Church are His agents and His **witnesses.** God uses us and will continue to use us to demonstrate Himself to the nations.

*Let **all the nations** be gathered together, And let the people be assembled..."**You are my witnesses**," says the Lord, and My servant whom I have chosen, That you may know and believe Me and understand that I am He. Before Me there was no God formed, Nor shall there be after Me. I, even I, am the Lord, and besides Me there is no Savior. I have declared and saved, I have proclaimed, and there was no foreign god among you; **therefore you are My witnesses,**" says the Lord, "that I am God..."* (Isaiah 43:9–12). (Emphasis added.)

*"...And that repentance and remission of sins **should be preached in His name** to all nations, beginning at Jerusalem. **And you are witnesses** of these things"* (Luke 24:47–48). (Emphasis added.)

*"But you shall receive power when the Holy Spirit has come upon you; and **you shall be witnesses to Me** and Jerusalem, and in all Judea and Samaria, **and to the end of the earth**"* (Acts 1:8). (Emphasis added.)

These verses are just a few examples of our roles as agents and witnesses of God's nature and character as His family members and protagonists in His Kingdom. Another one of our rulership roles in the Kingdom is to *provide a witness "testimony"* of our experiences with God to those who have yet to partake in such encounters.

Jesus did so.

Peter also did so by explaining this to the men of Judea at the time of the Holy Spirit's descent on the disciples during the feast of Pentecost.

"Men of Israel, hear these words: Jesus of Nazareth, a Man **attested by God** *to you* **by miracles, wonders, and signs** *which God did* **through Him** *in your midst, as you yourselves also know"* (Acts 2:22). (Emphasis added.)

"This Jesus God has raised up, **of which we are all witnesses** (Acts 2:32). (Emphasis added.)

Paul the Apostle did so. In Acts 26, we observe Paul the apostle *witnessing* to King Agrippa how it was that he became a Christian.

at midday, O king, along the road I saw a light from heaven, brighter than the sun, shining all around me and those who journeyed with me...Therefore, having obtained help from God, to this day I stand, **witnessing both to small and great**, *saying no other things other than those which the prophets and Moses said would come* (Acts 26: 13, 22). (Emphasis added.)

Roles as Witnesses

The world is waiting for witnesses who will offer life and hope to the people of the nations. Acting as witnesses is just one of our roles as members of God's ruling family. Besides doctrine, the world is essentially seeking firsthand testimonies regarding what encounters with God look and feel like. Sharing one's stories of God-man encounters provides the listener with hope that God is in fact real and alive.

For the earnest expectation of the creation eagerly waits for the revealing of the sons of God (Romans 8:19).

During my experience as an Administrative Law Judge, *witnesses* in my hearing rooms would serve the function of providing firsthand accounts to the listeners of what they saw, heard and sensed in a particular situation.

Likewise in the Church, we have observed that ministry is often more effective after eyewitness testimonies of personal meetings with God. In my experience during a decade in jail ministry, I discovered that the inmates desired the "real deal". Teaching Christian doctrine was essential but was much more powerful when linked with recalling a primary personal experience with the Father. The prisoners wanted to know all about our previous encounters with Him that resulted in answered prayers, interventions and miracles. Hearing about our personal encounters with the Lord inspired them to seek out the active presence of God to influence their own encounters in life.

As members of God's family, we are granted greater access to God that will hopefully result in a greater number of these *eyewitness* experiences.

Seeing then that we have a great High Priest who has passed through the heavens, Jesus the Son of God, **let us hold fast our confession.** *For we do not have a High Priest who cannot sympathize with our weaknesses, but was in all points tempted as we are yet without sin.* **Let us** *therefore* **come boldly to the throne of grace,** *that we may obtain mercy* **and find grace to help** *in time of need* (Hebrews 4:14–16). (Emphasis added.)

That which was from the beginning, which we have heard, which we have seen with our eyes, which we have looked upon, and our hands have handled, concerning the word of life-the life was manifested, and we have seen, **and bear witness,** *and declare to you that eternal life which was with the Father and was manifested to us-that which we have seen and heard we declare to you...* (1 John 1:1-3). (Emphasis added.)

And there shall be no more curse, but the throne of God and of the Lamb shall be in it, and His servants shall serve Him. **They** *shall see His face*, *and His name shall be on their foreheads* (Revelation 22:3). (Emphasis added.)

Witnesses are not able to give *meaningful* testimonies about relational experiences when their relationships are superficial or nonexistent. If we, as members of God's family, are to function in our roles as His **witnesses** to the world, this opportunity and responsibility require cultivating a close relationship with God the Father by means of His Son Jesus Christ. We can fake not having a relationship up to a certain point. However, people will eventually catch on as to whether we have a dynamic and flourishing relationship with our Father or not. We have been given a great privilege, which brings commensurate responsibility.

For everyone to whom much is given, from him much will be required; and to whom much has been committed, of him they will ask the more (Luke 12:48b).

When you think about it, all that is ultimately important in life is our relationship with God and with other people. These are the only things that last and even transcend physical death. Jesus explained this when He summarized the Ten Commandments in two commands, instructing that we love God with all of our heart, mind, soul and strength, and that we love our neighbors as ourselves.

Then one of them, a lawyer, asked Him a question, testing Him, and saying, "Teacher, which is the great commandment in the law?" Jesus said to him, "You shall love the Lord your God with all your heart, with all your soul, and with all your mind.' "This is the first and great commandment. And the second is like it: "You shall love your neighbor as yourself.' "On these two commandments hang all the Law and the Prophets" (Matthew 22: 35–40).

Beyond children, heirs and witnesses, I ascribe to the belief that the overcoming saints will play critical *roles* in carrying out God's soon-coming Kingdom on earth. Our future roles in God's Kingdom will become better defined as the desires of our hearts become fulfilled. When God informs us that it is His will to give us the desires of our hearts, we should ask ourselves the question of how those desires got there in the first place.

...For it is God who works in you both to will and to do for His good pleasure (Philippians 2:13).

Have you ever had a craving or yearning to become someone or do something? Have you ever inadvertently discovered a gifting or talent while carrying out a job, function or education? Have you ever enjoyed something so much that you would gladly do it without pay? God placed those desires of your heart within you. The personal talents you've discovered along your journey in life were a direct divine provision. Realizing that God has instilled personal talents in each of us helps us to understand our unique individual roles in His Kingdom.

For You formed my inward parts; You covered me in my mother's womb. For I will praise You, I am fearfully and wonderfully made; marvelous are Your works, and that my soul knows very well (Psalm 139:13–14).

Consider the following additional roles that we have yet to mention: The fivefold ministry list of roles that we find in the Ephesians chapter 4 mentions apostles, prophets, evangelists, pastors and teachers.

Christ also promises that if we are overcomers, we will sit with Him on His throne, which is designed for **rulers**.

As many as I love, I rebuke and chasten. Therefore be zealous and repent. Behold I stand at the door and knock. If anyone hears My voice and opens the door, I will come into him and dine with him, and he with Me. **To him who overcomes I will grant to sit with Me on My throne**, *as I also overcame and sat down with My Father on His throne* (Revelation 3:19–21). (Emphasis added.)

Rulers often serve as kings and priests.

And they sang a new song, saying: "...for You were slain, and have redeemed us to God by Your blood out of every tribe and tongue and people and nation, And have made us **kings and priests** *to our God;* **And we shall reign on the earth"** (Revelation 5:9–10). (Emphasis added.)

Rulers and kings are given crowns.

Behold, I am coming quickly! **Hold fast what you have**, *that no one may take* **your crown** (Revelation 3:11). (Emphasis added.)

Finally, **there is laid up for me the crown of righteousness**, *which the Lord, the righteous Judge, will give to me on that Day, and not to me only* **but also to all** *who have loved His appearing* (2 Timothy 4:8). (Emphasis added.)

We as *priests* will reign with Christ.

Blessed and holy is he who has part in the first resurrection. Over such the second death has no power, **but they shall be priests of God and of Christ**, *and shall reign with Him a thousand years* (Revelation 20:6). (Emphasis added.)

Rulers, kings and priests *need to serve others* with the *heart of a servant.*

So when he had washed their feet, taking his garments, and sat down again, he said to them, "Do you know what I have done to you? You call me Teacher and Lord, and you say well, for so I am. If I then, your Lord and Teacher, have washed your feet, you also are to wash one another's feet. For I have given you an example, that you should do as I have done to you. Most assuredly, I say to you, a servant is not greater than his master; nor is he who is sent greater then he who sent him. If you know these things, blessed are you if you do them (John 13:12–17).

And a servant of the Lord must not quarrel but be gentle to all, able to teach, patient, in humility correcting those who are in opposition... (2 Timothy 2:24–25).

Another role for the saints is that of **judges** of men and angels. Put on your seatbelt for this next verse:

*Do you not know that **the saints will judge** the world? And if the world will be judged by you are you unworthy to judge the smallest matters? Do you not know that **we shall judge angels**? How much more, things that pertain to this life?* (1 Corinthians 6:2–3). (Emphasis added.)

In addition, we are to be the **temple** of the Holy Spirit.

Or do you not know that your body is the temple of the Holy Spirit who is in you, whom you have from God, and you are not your own? For you were bought at a price; therefore glorify God in your body and your spirit, which are God's (1 Corinthians 6:19–20).

Also, we are to be **the abiding place** of the Father and the Son (John chapters 14, 15, 16, 17).

We are to be the **bride of the Lamb**.

Let us be glad and rejoice and give Him glory, for the **marriage of the Lamb** *has come, and* **His wife has made herself ready** (Revelation 19:7). (Emphasis added.)

Then I, John, saw the holy city, New Jerusalem, coming down out of heaven from God, **prepared as a bride** *adorned for her husband* (Revelation 21:2). (Emphasis added.)

The process of implementing God's plan for restoring these roles will be looked at more in depth in Chapter 7. For now, it is important to note that all the roles of the saints are consistent with the first two "R's" of God's original blueprint. *A genuine, vibrant relationship* between God and mankind gives man the privilege and responsibility to subdue *and rule* over His earthly creation. Our divinely provided identity as adopted children of the Most High God reveals our God-ordained gifts and talents designed for Kingdom service as His responsible agents, stewards, servants and witnesses.

Chapter 5

Rebellion: The Problem
You're Satan's Competition

The third "R" in the "5R" circular biblical blueprint deals with the problem currently confronting mankind: rebellion.

In chapter 2, we discussed the motive and the location of the original rebellion, which began in Heaven when Satan, a covering cherub close to the throne of God along with one third of the angels, fell into disobedience. (See Isaiah 14 and Ezekiel 28). Just like the old Ford automobile commercials in the 1970s, Satan thought he had "a better idea" and somehow got the crazy notion that angels were meant to have thrones. In Isaiah 14:13 Satan not only said that he will ascend into heaven, but also that he will exalt his throne above the stars of God.

This spiritual rebellion later invaded and penetrated the earth through mankind being deceived. (See Genesis 3). Satan's act of deception was accomplished when Satan called God's character into question first with the woman who later convinced the man to rebel against their Creator. The result ever since has been chaos, tears and pain here on earth.

When I was performing jail ministry as a chaplain, the inmates often asked me why Satan has such utter hatred for mankind. "What did I ever do to him to make him so angry and violent against me?", they would ask. I would respond that they— along with all human beings—are a potential threat to Satan's rebellious kingdom.

The more you think about it, the more it makes sense that Satan would launch a war of attrition against his competition of future human being rulers, kings, priests, judges of men and angels, wife of the Lamb, sons and daughters of God and co-heirs with Christ of the earth and its nations that we studied in chapter 4. God's plan for mankind's rulership destiny does not include sharing that responsibility with angels, much less fallen angels. Revelation 3:21 explains that thrones are meant for Father God, Jesus Christ as King of Kings and Lord of Lords and human overcomers. *Angels were never given the role of ruling* in God's plan. Their purpose is to worship God and serve as spiritual messengers, warriors and ministers to man. Fundamentally, *human beings are the ones* who collectively represent the fulfillment of God's blueprint plan for earthly rulership, which stands in direct opposition with Satan's desire to rule the earth.

The main battleground of the two competing spiritual kingdoms is located right here on this earth. The Second Temptation of Christ in Luke 4:5 took place on a mountain where the enemy shows Jesus, earth's soon-coming King, the world and its nations. Scripture speaks of most of the final battles of the end-time being fought on our earth. The reason Jesus came to earth was to destroy the works of the devil. It is a government replacement.

He who sins is of the devil, for the devil has sinned from the beginning. For this purpose the Son of God was manifested, that He might destroy the works of the devil. (1 John 3:8).

*For unto us a Child is born, unto us a Son is given; and the **government** will be upon His shoulder. And His name will be called Wonderful, Counselor, Mighty God, Everlasting Father, Prince of Peace. **Of the increase of His government** and peace there will be no end, **Upon the throne of David and over His kingdom**, to order it and establish it with judgment and justice* *from that time forward, even forever. The zeal of the Lord of hosts will perform this* (Isaiah 9:6). (Emphasis added.)

Even the Hebrew word for peace ("shalom") manifests itself "only when you destroy the authority that is connected to the chaos!" (Biltz 22-23).

Satan fully understands God's ultimate plan for the earth and its nations and wants to postpone, if not all together cancel, his inevitable judgment and defeat by attempting to discredit us in any way he can. In order to carry out his scheme, Lucifer must prove us unfit to govern and unworthy to judge men and angels, in spite of God's plans for us. That is why Satan accuses us day and night before the throne of God to prove that God was wrong about His destiny for us. The very name "Satan" means adversary. As our adversary, he continually accuses us before God.

Then I heard a loud voice saying in heaven, "Now salvation, and strength, and the kingdom of our God, and the power of His Christ have come, for the accuser of our brethren, who accused them before our God day and night, has been cast down..."(Revelation 12:10).

Satan attempts to achieve his never-ending quest to govern by influencing **the very same human vessels that God has selected to rule the earth and its nations**. Thus, since God's blueprint specifies that only human beings and not angels will rule the earth, Satan's only recourse is to employ *human agents* to continue to carry out his rebellion. To employ human agents, Lucifer must attempt to influence and even attempt to ultimately possess human flesh to control the course of events.

Human Rebellion

So what does human rebellion against God look like?

All rebellion, simply known as sin, is rooted in some form of disobedience against God.

Sin is serious—as serious as it gets.

The moment Adam and Eve disobeyed God, everything fell apart. Man was cursed and left to experience the natural result of rebellion against God: physical, emotional and spiritual death. Sin caused the death of God's Son. Sin will cause our physical death. It will also cause our spiritual death unless we separate ourselves from it.

Rebellion consists of man living his life independent of God while attempting to become a law unto himself. Rebellion is all about you getting your own way by doing what is right in your own eyes. You serve as your own god and act as the captain of your soul, subordinate to no one.

The Solution to Human Rebellion

Jesus only taught us one prayer, and it was the same prayer He taught His disciples when they asked Him how to pray: "The Lord's Prayer".

The petitions of "Thy kingdom come" and "Thy will be done" are the key tenets to the prayer *and the only solution* to the *problem of spiritual rebellion* here on earth. Asking that "God's will be done" is not merely a suggestion but rather a mandate intended for our salvation from the hand of our enemies. It is *the* mechanism of the forward advance of God's Kingdom being established on earth. Doing anything other than "Thy will be done" as Jesus taught in the Lord's Prayer puts us at cross-purposes with our Creator. We are either actively seeking and carrying out God's will in our lives, or we are not—there is no middle ground.

Our perfect role model for this type of complete obedience to Father God is Jesus Christ, who continually checked in with the Father to ensure that His will was being carried out in all circumstances.

Jesus said to them, *"My food is to do the will of Him who sent Me, and to finish His work"*(John 4:34).

Whenever God's fulfilled will is injected into a situation, the result will always be one of the nine fruits of the Spirit:

But the fruit of the Spirit is love, joy, peace, long-suffering, kindness, goodness, faithfulness, gentleness, self-control. Against such there is no law (Galatians 5:22-23).

Imagine the impact in local churches *if pastors were to begin to teach that the solution to God's problem of rebellion is to exercise "Thy will be done".* Imagine this powerful instruction in lieu of a powerless grace message that teaches grace serves only as forgiveness of sin and as a legal excuse for our continuing disobedience. Preaching "Thy will be done" as essential to the reestablishment of God's Kingdom here on earth and inside of us would probably not be considered a "seeker-sensitive" message. However, it would shift the focus away from entertaining immature believers to instead focus *on the desires of God's heart.*

Once we get serious about praying and implementing "Thy will be done", our world will inevitably change. It has to. Sin and rebellion will be obliterated in our lives and in the lives of others, and we all will finally experience the peaceable fruit of bringing the Kingdom to earth and to our personal lives:

*"...for the **kingdom of God** is not eating and drinking, but righteousness and peace and joy in the Holy Spirit"* (Romans 14:17). (Emphasis added.)

The harvest of spiritual fruit produced as a result of believers daily obeying God's perfect will in their individual lives would cause the world to finally sit up and begin to take notice. The power of God's Kingdom would be fully on display. (Just like what occurred in the San Diego County jail). Satan's chaotic rebellion would eventually be overturned and replaced with God's order and peace. In turn, as we exercise God's solution against the rebellion, ("Thy will be done") our relationship with the Father and our rulership over His creation will finally be restored.

"Thy will be done": the four ***most significant*** words in the Bible.

*For Yours is the kingdom **and the power** and glory forever. Amen* (Matthew 6:13). (Emphasis added.)

Chapter 6

Redemption: The Solution
You've Been Rescued

The fourth "R" word in God's perfect circular plan involves our Father providing **the perfect solution** to finally put an end to Satan's rebellion.

Our Heavenly Father outsmarted the rebellious fallen angel Lucifer by sending His divine/human Son, Jesus, to earth. Christ's assignment on earth was to serve in the role of mankind's Savior, Healer, Baptizer and soon-coming King. **His mission** was to present Himself as an atoning sacrificial offering **to reconcile fallen** mankind **back to Father God** (a *circular* process).

For Christ also suffered once for sins, the just for the unjust, **that He might bring us to God***, being put to death in the flesh but made alive by the Spirit,* (1 Peter 3:18). (Emphasis added.)

The carrying out of this mission required the introduction of God's heavenly government invading the earth to replace the established rebellious order entrenched in the world. Jesus Himself announces a spiritual governmental replacement on earth by means of the **redeeming** of mankind from the grasp of demonic slavery. As a result, God's children are **rescued and redeemed** (saved) **from the slavery of sin.**

"The time is fulfilled, and the kingdom of God is at hand. **Repent***, and believe in the gospel"* (Mark 1:15). (Emphasis added.)

*"The Spirit of the Lord is upon Me, because He has anointed Me to preach the gospel to the poor; He has sent Me to heal the brokenhearted, **to proclaim liberty to the captives** and recovery of sight to the blind, **to set at liberty those who are oppressed**; to proclaim the acceptable year of the Lord"* (Luke 4:18–19).

*To open their eyes, **in order to turn them** from darkness to light, **and from the power of Satan to God**, that they may receive forgiveness of sins **and an inheritance** among those who are sanctified by faith in Me* (Acts 26:18). (Emphasis added.)

*For if we have been united together in the likeness of His death, certainly we also shall be in the likeness of His resurrection, knowing this, that our old man was crucified with Him, that the body of sin might be done away with, **that we should no longer be slaves of sin**. For he who has died **has been freed from sin**. Likewise you also, reckon yourselves to be dead indeed to sin, but alive to God in Christ Jesus our Lord. **Therefore do not let sin reign in your mortal body, that you should obey its lusts. For sin shall not have dominion over you** for you are not under law **but under grace*** (Romans 6: 5–7,11–12, 14). (Emphasis added.)

What exactly does it mean to be ***redeemed?***

By definition, to be redeemed means to repurchase an item, ***to buy*** or ***win something back*** or ***to liberate by payment***.

You can only redeem something that you ***earlier*** possessed and ***later*** lost.

What we as God's children ***earlier possessed*** through our original parents was a ***relationship with Father God (eternal life)*** prior to Satan's rebellion invading the earth.

Correspondingly, God officially delegated to our original parents that they—and later on, we—exercise dominion and stewardship over our earthly paradise. We can see the Father's perfect blueprint as He originally intended it by simply reviewing the first two chapters of Genesis.

Tragically, we lost it all due to our first human parents allowing themselves to be deceived by agreeing with the lies of Satan regarding our Father's character. (See Genesis chapter 3.)

We lost God. Thus, we lost our eternal life. (See John 17:3.)

We also lost our gifted inheritance: paradise on earth.

We had it all.

We lost it all.

Human nature is such that we often do not appreciate what we have until the moment we no longer have it.

Fortunately for us, our Father's strategic plan of redemption includes *buying us back from Satan* (redemption). *This is made possible through Christ voluntarily giving up His life as an obedient atoning sacrifice to the Father.* Jesus offering His life in place of ours assuages God's ire caused by our participation in Satan's rebellion of disobedience. As a result of the Son's obedient atoning death, we were saved from spiritual death and *reconciled back* (redeemed) to our *Father*. *Eventually, we will also be returned back to* our *earthly destiny* of rulership over the nations of the earth (a *circular* experience).

In summary: *Redemption consists of us returning back home to our Father and eventually back home to our earth.*

"The soul who sins shall die" (Ezekiel 18:4).

Bless the Lord O my soul...Who **redeems your life** *from destruction (Psalm 103:1,4).* (Emphasis added.)

Or do you not know that your body is the temple of the Holy Spirit who is in you, whom you have from God, and you are not your own? **For you were bought at a price;(redeemed)** *therefore glorify God in your body and your spirit* **which are God's** (1Corinthians 6:19–20). (Emphasis and key word added.)

And they sang a new song, saying: "You are worthy to take the scroll, and to open its seals; For You were slain, **and have redeemed us to God** *by Your blood Out of every tribe and tongue and people and nation,* **And have made us kings and priests to our God; and we shall reign on the earth"** (Revelation 5:9–10). (Emphasis added.)

The Purpose of Redemption

So what is God attempting to accomplish by redeeming us? Does He have a larger goal in mind?

Most **Gentile** Christians today would likely define **being saved or redeemed** as being allowed to enter Heaven when they die, thus avoiding judgment and hell. Their focus is more on a **location** as the goal—a **Greek, linear** type of thinking.

We Gentile Evangelicals launch ourselves out into the world by asking the unsaved if they happened to die today, **where** would they go?

Having grown up in parochial school, I was taught that eternal life meant that when you physically die, you relocate to Heaven as a disembodied spirit to stay forever. Eternal life according to the nuns was *location* centered, i.e. Heaven=eternal life (a *linear* and Greek concept by design).

I stand by my claim that most Gentile Christians (Protestant and Catholic) still believe exactly the same parochial teaching that I was taught.

Recently, I observed a local church's high school youth group at the beach approaching beach goers with the question, "If you were to die tonight, *where would you go?*"

I contend it is the wrong question to ask.

A Hebrew *circular/cyclical* Kingdom question would go something like this: "Sir, if you were to die this evening, *who* would be waiting for you?" or "With whom would you meet up?

These type of Kingdom questions help change *the focus* of the inquiry very quickly. The focus of the people to whom the Kingdom question is addressed would shift from *an incorrectly perceived goal of a location to the correct goal of a Person*.

The two goals are not the same.

For example, *to be redeemed or saved in the Hebrew mind signifies something altogether different than to the linear-oriented Greek mind.*

There is only one small problem: The Greek concept is not what the Bible teaches.

Eternal life as described in the Bible depicts an *abiding fellowship-relationship* that involves knowing God in a visceral fashion.

"I will dwell in them and walk among them. I will be their God, and they shall be My people" (2 Corinthians 6:16).

Where and how does *the Bible* define eternal life?

Only in one verse:

*And **this is eternal life**, that they **may know You**, the only true God, and Jesus Christ whom You have sent* (John 17:3). (Emphasis added.)

Studying the definition of eternal life leads to the conclusion that if eternal life signifies **knowing God and His Son**, then eternal life cannot be a "what" nor a "where" but rather must be a **"Who!"**

If Christ states in John 10:10 that He came that we may have "life" and have it abundantly, then "knowing God" as seen in John 17:3 must include the idea that **we can possess eternal life** in increasing measures and amounts in the here and now. These measures and amounts can grow or diminish **based on the degree that we seek out** His fellowship and abiding in us.

Draw near to God and He will draw near to you (James 4:8).

Hebrews typically understand that the **notion of salvation/redemption involves being rescued from their enemies** and **reunited with their Heavenly Father** as we see in the prophesy of Zacharias, the father of John the Baptist in Luke 1:67–77. The Hebrew focus expressed by Zacharias concentrated more on a **re-establishment of relationship with God the Father**—reflecting a return ("aliyah") to the beginning—a **circular** type of thinking.

The verses below illustrate this perspective:

Now his father Zacharias was filled with the Holy Spirit, and prophesied, saying: "Blessed is the Lord God of Israel, for He has visited and redeemed His people, And has raised up a horn of salvation for us In the house of His servant David, As He spoke by the mouth of His holy prophets, Who have been since the world began, That we should be saved from our enemies and from the hand of all who hate us, To perform the mercy promised to our fathers and to remember His holy covenant, the oath which He swore to our father Abraham: To grant us that we, Being delivered from the hand of our enemies, Might serve Him without fear, In holiness and righteousness before Him all the days of our life. And you, child, will be called the prophet of the Highest; For you will go before the face of the Lord to prepare His ways, To give knowledge of salvation to His people by the remission of their sins... (Luke 1:67–77). (Emphasis added.)

What we really need to ask ourselves is which of the two points of view (Greek vs. Hebrew) does the Scripture seem to emphasize?

I proffer the notion that the Bible hones in on the concept of *redemption* as a stepping stone to a *much greater objective* than just achieving a change of locations. Simply changing locations *does not address* the spiritual rebellion problem that God has on His hands. God has to deal with an ongoing problematic invasion of Satan's spiritual rebellion entrenched on earth and fortified within us. When our original parents tragically invited this spiritual rebellion to become a part of us, we, as God's children, lost our eternal life. That is to say *we stopped knowing Him* as described in John 17:3. Additionally, we, His children, *lost our inheritance of earthly rulership* under the headship of God.

Abandoning our earthly inheritance and existing as disembodied spirits in the spiritual world is not part of God's original blueprint plan. We are not supposed to be relocated *to a spiritual place to be with God*. He was *already* on the earth with mankind. He spoke to us. He spent time with us. He walked in the cool of the day right there in the Garden—on Earth. He trusted Adam with all the beasts of the field and birds of the air to see what he would name them. (See Genesis chapters 2–3.)

When God speaks of redemption, He is by definition referring *to returning back* to what was *earlier* planned for us. I do not see any verses in the Bible describing God ever having changed His mind concerning the marvel He created when He declared all of creation to be *"very good"* back in Genesis 1:31.

God's first and foremost *objective of redeeming His children is to restore our eternal life*.

"And this is eternal life, *that they may know You*, the only true God, and Jesus Christ whom you have sent" (John 17:3). (Emphasis added.)

Knowing Father God experientially in the here and now is eternal life. We can have it now, in the present moment!

*"I will be a **Father** to you, and you shall be **My sons and daughters**, says the Lord Almighty"* (2 Corinthians 6:18). (Emphasis added.)

We need *to return back* to our Father.

*"I am the way, the truth, and the life. No one comes **to the Father** except through Me"* (John 14:6). (Emphasis added.)

So, what does *God's goal* for us being *redeemed* back to Him even look like?

I maintain that the experience of salvation/redemption is similar to receiving a full-ride scholarship. It is a free gift that we cannot nor should not try to earn.

For by grace you have been saved through faith, and that not of yourselves; it is the gift of God, not of works, lest anyone should boast (Ephesians 2:8–9).

When we repent (change the way we formerly thought and acted) for being in sin against God's will, we are first forgiven and liberated of our sin-driven guilt and shame through the obedient blood sacrifice of Messiah Jesus on the cross. Jesus, as our sin-forgiving Savior, provides us with the freedom from our past and present guilt. This free gift of initial salvation is purchased through Yeshua (Jesus of Nazareth) obediently offering His life in place of ours to satisfy the death penalty of sin.

After we are forgiven of our **guilt,** we are then **liberated** (redeemed) from the **compulsion** to continue sinning by being transformed and made new into His **image** through the power of the Holy Spirit. This results in **union** with God by our becoming **His dwelling place,** finally providing the solution to the problem of spiritual rebellion within us.

*He who sins is of the devil, for the devil has sinned from the beginning. For this purpose the Son of God was manifested, that **He might destroy the works of the devil** (1 John 3:8). (Emphasis added.)*

*But we all, with unveiled face, beholding as in a mirror the glory of the Lord, are being transformed into the **same image** from glory to glory, just as by the Spirit of the Lord (2 Corinthians 3:18). (Emphasis added.)*

*And what agreement has the temple of God with idols? For **you are the temple** of the living God. As God has said: **I will dwell in them** and walk among them I will be their God, and they shall be My people"*(2 Corinthians 6:16). (Emphasis added.)

*For the **grace of God** that **brings salvation** has appeared to all men, **teaching us** that, denying ungodliness and worldly lusts, **we should live soberly, righteously, and godly** in the present age, looking for the blessed hope and glorious appearing of our great God and Savior Jesus Christ, who gave Himself for us, **that He might redeem us from every lawless deed and purify for Himself His own special people**, zealous for good works* (Titus 2:11–14). (Emphasis added.)

Sin always causes death. (See Romans 6:23.)

The soul who sins shall die (Ezekiel 18:4).

After we are first saved (redeemed) from spiritual death, we are then saved from physical death at our bodily resurrection.

Blessed and holy is he who has part in the first resurrection. Over such the second death has no power…(Revelation 20:6).

Yet our initial salvation/redemption is simply the ***beginning of our journey towards eternal life.***

Initial salvation is a gift of an opportunity to lay hold of eternal life.

Fight *that good fight of faith**, lay hold on eternal life**, to which you were also called…* (1 Timothy 6:12). (Emphasis added.)

"Enter by the narrow gate; for wide is the gate and broad is the way that leads to destruction, and there are many who go in by it. "Because narrow is the gate and difficult is the way

*which leads **to life** and there are **few** who find it* (Matthew 7:13–14). (Emphasis added.)

Jesus proclaimed that He was sent by God to earth in order that we would have **eternal life**.

*"For God so loved the world that He gave His only begotten Son, that whoever believes in Him should not perish but have **everlasting life*** (John 3:16). (Emphasis added.)

*"The thief does not come except to steal, and to kill, and to destroy. **I have come that they may have life, and that they may have it more abundantly"*** (John 10:10). (Emphasis added.)

Redemption/salvation is *a gift of an opportunity* to live, to find and to continue to grow *in experiencing eternal life (knowing God)* in the here and now.

Eternal life consists of *knowing* God. Not just knowing about Him, but rather knowing Him on an intimate level. It is something that we must give ourselves to. The reality is that we are falling in love with a Person, a Divine Person. *Our one opportunity* to attain eternal life occurs while we are physically alive here on the earth. We are the ones who set the limits on how well we know Him. We are the ones who can open up the spigots, close them partially down or shut them off entirely. How much eternal life we take in is up to us. If we fail to take advantage of our life's singular chance *to know* the Father and the Son, there are dramatic eternal consequences that we cannot change after we die.

The apostle Paul explained to Timothy that *eternal life*, **God's goal of redemption** and restoration, *must be laid hold of* (1 Timothy 6:12). This entails *learning the sound* of both Our

Father's and Jesus' voices. It also entails **responding** by doing "Thy will be done" found in the Lord's Prayer.

Obeying God is not legalism. The carrying out of God's will is actually **the key** to eternal life.

*"**My food is to do the will of Him** who sent Me, and to finish His work"* (John 4:34). (Emphasis added.)

*If you love Me, **keep** my commandments* (John 14:15). (Emphasis added.)

*"I am the good Shepherd; And I know My sheep, and am known by My own." "My sheep **hear My voice, and I know them, and they follow Me**. "And I give them **eternal life**, and they shall never perish, neither shall anyone snatch them out of My hand"* (John 10:14, 27–28). (Emphasis added.)

*Now by this **we know that we know Him**, if we keep His commandments* (1 John 2:3–4). (Emphasis added.)

It bears repeating: *"And this is eternal life, **that they may know You**, the only true God, and Jesus Christ whom You have sent"* (John 17:3). (Emphasis added.)

Our redemption **begins** the "getting to know Him" process. Our redemption is a free gift that can be expanded on or squandered. It is up to us which way the process ultimately pans out. This free gift requires our time and investment. The Hebrews had to spend 40 years in the desert getting to know God by learning to trust Him **after** their redemption from 432 years of captivity under the yoke of Pharaoh.

*"And you shall remember that the Lord your God led you all the way these 40 years in the wilderness, **to humble you and test you to know what was in your heart, whether you would***

keep His commandments or not. So he humbled you, allowed you to hunger, and fed you with manna which you did not know nor did your fathers know, that He might make you know that man shall not live by bread alone; but man lives by every word that proceeds from the mouth of the Lord. For the Lord your God is bringing you into a good land, a land of brooks of water, of fountains and springs, that flow out of valleys and hills (Deuteronomy 8:2–3, 7).

For example, if you had received a free, all expenses paid scholarship to attend medical school, what would be expected of you? Wouldn't the reasonable expectation be *a degree* demonstrating your dedication, qualification and persistence? *The ultimate goal is getting the degree*—not the student brandishing the scholarship document, claiming that *the intent* of the scholarship had already been completed.

If we think like *linear* Greeks, our understanding is that salvation/redemption is the beginning *and end* of the story since it's *location*-oriented. With a Greek linear approach, the only "knowing" required to be saved/redeemed involves reciting head knowledge facts listed in the "Four Steps to Salvation" booklet. Salvation at typical evangelical crusades *often* (not always) involves more "Greek" mental and verbal acknowledgement of "gnosis" (head knowledge) rather than Hebrew, heart-dedicated, experiential knowledge on a personal level. In general, Greeks *think* their faith and worship through reason, while Hebrews *live* their faith by trusting God, thus producing a firm and lasting relationship.

Our job is *to experience* God our Father and His Son on a Deuteronomy 8:2-7 level. God will test where are our hearts are. He must test us before once again entrusting His children to rule the earth under Jesus the Messiah King. Too much is at stake.

Even in our jail ministry, we would teach the inmates this same concept that the gift of initial salvation/redemption was akin to an opportunity comparable to receiving a musical instrument such as a fine classical guitar as a free gift. The *free* gift from God of **salvation/ redemption** cannot be earned by obeying the dead works, rituals and observances of the Law of Moses. We understand that. As Christians, we can explain that to the unsaved in about three minutes.

However, what many of us do not understand is *that the purpose of the scholarship* in this musical instrument example *was to result in being able to play the instrument*! The free gift of the guitar came with a user's manual in order to produce the intended result. We have to actually open the music book and practice our scales. Every day. And the more we practice, the better we get at it. With repetition, we develop skills and become adept at them. Again, *the point of the scholarship in the first place* is to produce *a degree* reflecting a highly trained, qualified graduate. It is not a question of earning initial salvation. We cannot earn a free gift. The question is what was the point in our receiving the free gift in the first place?

In our Kingdom redemption model, God's free gift of salvation/redemption was provided with the purpose of pleasing the Gift Giver (our Heavenly Father) by becoming proficient in learning how to fall in love with Him and learn what "Thy will be done" from the Lord's Prayer looks like. This can only come by investing our time (reading the user's manual i.e. the Bible) and by our obedient efforts to produce the results sought by the Gift Giver. (See Matthew 25.)

At the end of our time here on earth, we will either be *qualified* to play the "freely gifted guitar" or to "practice medicine", etc. or we will not. We are being trained *now* for our present and future Kingdom roles. We are being trained to know His voice and leadings. This takes time and practice. There is no substitute for the time and effort required to acquire this qualification of competence. The rewards to the saints in the Book of Revelation are given *only* to the overcomers.

*I beseech you therefore, brethren, by the mercies of God, **that you present your bodies a living sacrifice**, holy, acceptable to God, **which is your reasonable service**. And do not be conformed to this world, but **be transformed by the renewing of your mind, that you may prove what is that good and acceptable and perfect will of God** (Romans 12: 1–2).*

*"**He who overcomes shall inherit all things**, and I will be his God and he shall be My son* (Revelation 21:7). (Emphasis added.)

*"And behold, I am coming quickly, **and My reward is with Me**, to give to everyone **according to his work*** (Revelation 22:12). (Emphasis added.)

What if we were to blow all of this off as simply trying to save oneself through "works", as a family relative of mine recently proposed? Then I would say we would have entirely missed the point of what our Father's plan is all about and what He has set out to accomplish.

It would be well worth our time to review the two parables in Matthew 25. We need to ask ourselves whether those parables were directed towards believers or to the unsaved.

Unbelievers are not given "talents" as used in the context of the parable. *Unsaved* "virgins" would not have lamps and oil while awaiting the arrival of the bridegroom.

In the context of these parables, Jesus' message is directed to the saved. If we are thinking like linear Greeks, this parable does not make a whole lot of sense within our Greek linear framework of salvation/redemption as a "ticket" to heaven.

For example, I was actually taught in Bible college that the Gospels, especially the Gospel of Matthew, were not relevant to the "post cross" Gentile experience. The instructor said that the principles Jesus cited at the Sermon on the Mount in the book of Matthew were only applicable to the Jews. Wow! Really?

During our next class break out in the hallway, I sarcastically mentioned to my student colleagues (who happened to mostly be ordained Christian pastors) that I was going to borrow a razorblade so I could remove the four "pre-cross, Jewish-only" Gospels from my Bible. I also sarcastically announced that I would be graduating earlier than they would since I'm not Jewish and could therefore skip those Gospel classes in my studies.

I am sorry, but that type of Gentile/Greek thinking is simply not how God's Kingdom works. Greek, linear thinking often forces us to "cherry pick" the parts of the Bible we find most acceptable and that fit within our Hellenized Gospel model.

*"For I have not shunned to declare to you **the whole counsel of God"** (Acts 20:27). (Emphasis added.)

Look, the individual who received one talent from his lord *had an opportunity* to invest and to increase the single talent that had been freely given to him. The fact is this servant with the single talent buried it. He, *unlike the others who were fruitful and productive with the talents they had been freely given*, ended up being called wicked and lazy by his lord. Not only that, the one talent given to him that he buried was taken away and given to another servant who had been faithful to increase his particular gift. The wicked, lazy servant's ultimate destiny was outer darkness where there would be weeping and gnashing of teeth. Not a fun place. The absence of the presence of God forms the darkness. If you want to be location-focused and attempt to rationalize that outer darkness is not the same as the lake of fire, ask yourself this question first: Why is outer darkness known for its weeping and gnashing of teeth?

My theory is the following: What is your physical reaction when you possess something valuable, and due to your lack of care and/or diligence, it slips from your grasp? Later, you discover that the lost item (or relationship) was the key to your joy, completeness, and satisfying fulfillment. How do you react when you lose something precious over which you had a chance to influence, nurture, develop or expand? When it has happened to me, I recall clenching my fists and gnashing my teeth while proclaiming all the while: "I had it in my hand and I lost it!"

Understandably, outer darkness produces that same reaction from those who are there. They had something of great value in their grasp, and through their lack of seriousness and diligence, they are now in a place of darkness. They are away from the life and light of the presence of God, weeping and gnashing their teeth. It could have been so different. And the worst part is that they can't go back to fix it.

"Coulda", woulda", shoulda" for the rest of time.

Not a pleasant thought.

*"**Enter** by the narrow gate; for wide is the gate and broad is the way that leads to destruction, and there are many who go in by it. **Because narrow is the gate and difficult is the way which leads to life, and there are few who find it** (Matthew 7:13–14). (Emphasis added.)*

As we see Jesus explaining in the verses from Matthew above, *life has to be entered into.* Whether you use the verb to "lay hold of" or "to enter", both Jesus and Paul understood that *our salvation/redemption is just the beginning of the journey* towards *knowing* God relationally and intimately again. This "laying hold of" eternal life and "entering" into life requires our most committed diligence.

*But also for this very reason, **giving all diligence**, add to your faith virtue, to virtue knowledge, to knowledge self-control, to self-control perseverance, to perseverance godliness, to godliness brotherly kindness, and to brotherly kindness love. For if these things are yours and abound, you will be neither barren nor unfruitful **in the knowledge of our Lord Jesus Christ*** (2 Peter 1:5–8). (Emphasis added.)

*Therefore, brethren**, be even more diligent to make your call and election sure**, for if you do these things you will never stumble* (2 Peter1:10). (Emphasis added.)

So what does diligence look like?

All of the rewards to the "overcomers" that we see in the book of Revelation are given to those who "overcome".

Why was Paul the Apostle in his letter to the Philippians (Philippians 3:12) "pressing on" that he "may lay hold of" that for which Christ Jesus also "laid hold of" him? What would be the point of all those action verbs if redemption/salvation only meant relocation to Heaven? Wasn't Paul already saved/redeemed? Why all the physical effort of "pressing towards the goal"?

Was Paul confused as to God's ultimate goal in his second letter to Timothy when he spoke of "fighting the good fight" and having "finished the race" while "keeping the faith"? I thought salvation/redemption couldn't be earned through works.

Or perhaps Paul the Apostle understood that **there was something more to attain** beyond initial salvation/redemption per the Father's blueprint?

The answer is Paul did indeed understand that there was something beyond the free gift of the salvation scholarship opportunity. That free gift at the cross was to enable us to "*lay hold of*" and "*enter*" into our own personal dynamic relationship with our Divine Father *so that we may personally experience that which is called Eternal Life*. Eternal life *is* the blueprint goal. Eternal Life *is* a **Person**, a Divine Person. It is a **circular** experience.

Getting to know God intimately is not an "add water and shake proposition". It requires everything we have. Our Father loves us with a jealous love and will not share us. When the Father gave everything for us in the form of the atoning death of His Son Jesus Christ, the question He needs to know is whether we are prepared to give everything we have back to Him. (See the story of the rich young ruler in Luke 18:18.) Indeed, personally knowing Father God and Jesus Christ requires an entirely different level of commitment on our part than what we may be used to. We will be asked to give an account to our Creator on **how** we spent our time, investments and commitments. In other words, we will have to explain whether we were just living life for ourselves or for our Lord.

You shall love the Lord with all your heart, with all your soul, and with all your mind. This is the first and great commandment (Matthew 22:37–38).

So then each of us shall give account of himself to God (Romans 14:12).

Therefore we make it our aim, whether present or absent, to be well pleasing to Him. For we must all appear before the judgment seat of Christ, that each one may receive the things done in the body, according to what he has done, whether good or bad. Knowing, therefore, the terror of the Lord, we persuade men... (2 Corinthians 5:9–11).

How about the cited verse below for a summation?

*I beseech you therefore, brethren, by the mercies of God, that you **present your bodies a living sacrifice**, holy, acceptable to God, which is your reasonable service* (Romans 12:1). (Emphasis added.)

Can you now see how Platonic, Greek, *linear* thinking influenced the Church early on by teaching that God's ultimate goal *was to relocate us* from *earthly* "Point A" to *celestial* "Point B" has little relevance in the larger scheme of God's perfect blueprint plan? Physical relocation from earth to Heaven *as a goal* reflects Western, Greek, Platonic, Gnostic thinking.

Walking away from the power of Satan *and returning to our Father* is "Eternal Life" (Acts 26:18). Verbs are quite prominent and significant in the Hebrew language. The Hebrew approach to clarity is "show me your deeds as evidence of your creed".

Contemporary Greek, Gentile, linear Biblical perspective often views Biblical command verbs in Scripture as "works" in an attempt *to earn* initial salvation/redemption.

This *Platonic linear perspective* misses the whole point of the Father's Hebrew *circular/cyclical* blueprint. It is a *distortion* of the Biblical Hebraic message. The dictionary meaning of *to distort* something means *to twist* something out of its original, natural shape. Platonic *linear* perspective twists the significance of the Biblical Hebrew *circular/cyclical* message out of its original, natural shape. The dictionary definition of *to pervert* someone or something means *to divert* someone or something to a wrong end or purpose. It also means to twist the meaning or sense of something ("twist". "pervert". *Merriam-Webster.com*, Merriam-Webster, 2015. Web. 11 November 2015).

Unchallenged distortions (twistings) end up being unquestioned perversions (diversions).

Jesus came to earth to give us eternal life as defined in John 17:3 below. Eternal life is a relationship with God, *not a relocation.*

*"I have come that **they may have life** and have it abundantly"* (John 10:10). (Emphasis added.)

*"I am the way, the truth, **and the life**. No one comes **to the Father** except by Me"* (John 14:6). (Emphasis added.)

*"And this is **eternal life**, that they **may know You**, the **only true God**, and **Jesus Christ** whom You have sent"* (John 17:3). (Emphasis added.)

So the question now becomes, ***How** does one "enter" or "lay hold of" the goal of the scholarship—eternal life?*

This question is addressed and answered in the next chapter as we proceed to examine the 5th "R" word in the 5 "R" circle.

Chapter 7

Restoration: You, the New!
A Completed Circle

Restoration is the 5th and final "R" that completes God's circular blueprint and eventually comes around full circle to link up with the 1st "R" of **relationship**.

Although the *redemption/salvation* experience can be instantaneous, *restoration* tends to be a lifelong process. God **restores** our intimate relationship with Him through moment-by-moment, step-by-step series of experiences.

God is in the business of relationship restoration. God's goal of restoration is a personal invitation into His presence. As the Father begins the ***circular restoration process of relationship*** with us, we begin to understand that ***we must actively participate and invest*** the very essence of our lives into the pursuit of relationally ***knowing*** God. As we move first, God responds. As we invite His presence, He shows up.

Draw near to God and He will draw near to you (James 4:8).

A clear example of God's desire to ***restore*** **relationships** is the journey of the Israelites from Egypt back to Canaan. The Israelites had been Pharaoh's slaves for over four centuries, and as a result, they had lost their relationship with God. God's purpose in allowing their wandering 40 years in the Sinai was to test their motivations. During this time, they were given multiple opportunities to lean on God, to trust Him as provider and protector and to identify themselves as His children. They needed to get reacquainted, and their relationship needed to be ***restored***. A few of them were successful. Most were not.

*And you shall remember that **the Lord your God led you all the way** these 40 years in the wilderness, **to humble you and test you, to know what was in your heart**, whether you would keep his Commandments or not* (Deuteronomy 8:2). (Emphasis added.)

*For who, having heard, rebelled? Indeed, was it not all who came out of Egypt, led by Moses? Now with whom was He angry 40 years? Was it not with those who sinned, whose corpses fell in the wilderness? And to whom did He swear **that they would not enter His rest**, but to those **who did not obey**? So we see that they could not enter in because of **unbelief*** (Hebrews 3:16–19). (Emphasis added.)

*Therefore, **since a promise remains of entering His rest**, let us fear lest any of you seem to have come short of it. For indeed the gospel was preached to us as well as them; but the word which they heard did not profit them, **not being mixed with faith** in those who heard it. **For we who have believed do enter that rest**...*(Hebrews 4:1–3). (Emphasis added.)

Relationship Despite Circumstances

Another example of God's desire to have a genuine relationship with us is found in the book of Job. After 42 agonizing chapters, the upshot was that Job was *restored* not only to his original position and status, but all of his property losses were also replenished with a double portion. The Father blessed him with the same number of children as he had earlier. God proved Himself faithful and trustworthy just as Job did in the long run. And his experience *was* a long run.

Proving the quality of the relationship between Job and God was the whole point of the book. Job's challenging experiences were a process of getting *to know* God in a completely different and more profound way.

This same drama of testing mankind's motives towards God has a *circular* component, playing itself out over and over again in the historical accounts of the Bible. The same applies to us in contemporary times. Each of us has our own "Job story" experience to one degree or another. *The central question* in the debate between God and Satan is if man *will be faithful, loyal and obedient in carrying out God's will in every circumstance of our lives based on the quality of our relationship with Him.* God and Satan both insist on knowing whether the steadfastness of our pledge of love and loyalty to God the Father and His Son, Jesus Christ, is sincere—come what may. We need to know the answer to that question as well. Eternity—based on the answer—hangs in the balance. Our very destinies also hang in the balance.

That which is has already been, and what is to be has already been; and God requires an account of what is past (Ecclesiastes 3:15)

Learning Obedience

Restoring relationship means coming to *know* the Lord intimately, resulting in us lovingly submitting to the Father and carrying out His will. *Doing His will* is a *reflection, evidence and measuring rod of the quality of our relationship* with Him.

Learning obedience through restoration is a journey and a process—it is the **very reason** we were initially saved.

*Though He was a Son, yet **He learned obedience** by the things which He suffered. And having been perfected, **He became the author of eternal salvation to all who obey Him**...*(Hebrews 5:8–9). (Emphasis added.)

121

*Now by this **we know** that **we know Him**, **if we keep His commandments**. He who says, "I know Him," and does not keep His Commandments, is a liar, and the truth is not in Him* (1 John 2:3–4). (Emphasis added.)

*Circumcision is nothing and uncircumcision is nothing, **but keeping the commandments of God is what matters*** (1 Corinthians 7:19). (Emphasis added.)

God's Goals of Restoration

As we discussed in Chapter 3, as we begin to engage in the *circular* process of *relational restoration* to our Father, He begins to reveal that He is the source of our *identity, protection and provision*. And when we begin to identify ourselves as *members of His family*, He begins to reveal His *goals and roles* for us within the blueprint for His Kingdom.

We spelled out in Chapter 3 God's **4** main *goals* for mankind of *dwelling, union, image and rest* that are designed to bring about the restoration of relationship with Him, completing a *circular* process. The nature of these goals involves a *personal* dimension for each individual.

However, I maintain that Father God *additionally seeks to complete* a *corporate* goal as well as individual goals for this epic season in which we live. It applies to unifying the Hebrew and Gentile communities into a single group under the headship of Yeshua.

Paul the Apostle, in his letters to the Galatians (chapter 3) and Ephesians (chapters 2 and 3), discusses the concept of what *"one new man" in Christ* looks like. God the Father is a builder. Based on His divine *circular* blueprint, He is putting the finishing touches on His construction of what Paul described as the "whole building being fitted together." This divine building has *Yeshua* as the *cornerstone*, the *Hebrew* apostles and prophets as the *foundation* and the Jewish/Gentile household members as "the Holy Temple in the Lord" in whom we are being *built together for a dwelling place of God* in the Spirit" (Ephesians 2:21-22).

Wow! Try to wrap your mind and arms around that one.

Paul also refers to a *mystery of God* in Ephesians chapter 3. It was a mystery not known by the sons of men of other ages. This mystery, per Paul, had been revealed by the Spirit to Christ's holy apostles and prophets (all Hebrews except for Luke). Paul's job was to make sure all would be able to see the *"fellowship of the mystery"* that from the beginning of the ages was hidden in God who created all things through Christ. The revelation of the Father's mystery in Christ is that *we Gentiles* are being invited *through Yeshua* into the *household of God* as *fellow heirs* of the same body and partakers of the promise in Christ through the Gospel.

We can get a glimpse of what Paul is revealing by adding the third chapter of Galatians to the mix. Paul explains that Christ has redeemed all from the curse of the Law by our being justified by faith in Him. The idea is that Scripture foresaw that God intended to justify the Gentiles through their faith in Christ just as Abraham was justified by his faith in God. Thus, through our being justified by our faith in Christ, *we Gentiles are now designated as sons of Abraham and heirs to the promise.*

Now to Abraham and his Seed were the promises made. He does not say, " And to seeds," as of many, but as of one, "And to your seed," who is Christ (Galatians 3:16).

What promises?, you may ask. God promised Abraham that he would be made into a great and blessed nation, and that through him, all nations would be blessed (Genesis 12:1-3; Galatians 3:8). This same promise now inures to all Gentiles who have "put on Christ." Paul goes on to explain the connection that *if* we are "Christ's, then we are Abrahams's seed, and heirs according to the promise" (Galatians 3:27, 29).

For as many of you as were baptized into Christ have put on Christ (Galatians 3:27).

And if you are Christ's, then you are Abraham's seed, and heirs according to the promise (Galatians 3:29).

And you are Christ's and Christ is God's (1 Corinthians 3:23).

Part of the mystery revealed through the Hebrew prophets and the apostles involves the *convergence* through Christ, the Seed of Abraham, of two groups of distinct cultures—Hebrew and Greek.

There is neither Jew nor Greek, *there is neither slavery nor free, there is neither male nor female;* **for you are all one in Christ Jesus** (Galatians 3:28). (Emphasis added.)

Prior to the convergence of these two people groups mentioned in Ephesians chapter 2 and Galatians chapter 3, Paul describes the uncircumcised Gentiles of the flesh as aliens from the commonwealth of Israel and strangers from the covenants of promise having no hope without God. Though the Gentiles were once far off, they are **now** brought near by the blood of Christ. Yeshua plays the role of a magnet bringing two disparate groups together as "one new man" in Christ, our Peace (Ephesians 2:14–15). **Unity with Jesus** breaks down the wall of separation and puts to death the enmity between these two people groups.

All of this was designed by the Father to create in Himself *through Christ "one new man"*, reconciling the two previously separated groups of the Father's children. As this reconciliation occurs, it paves the way for the Father's ultimate goal of bringing *all* of His children *back to Him* to finally come to fruition. Access to the Father is available *to all* through Christ by one Spirit (a *circular* process).

For through Him we both have access by one Spirit *to the Father* (Ephesians 2:18). (Emphasis added.)

We Gentiles now have a new identity through Yeshua, Jesus Christ of Nazareth. We Gentiles are no longer strangers and foreigners. We are *now fellow citizens* with the saints *and members of the household* of God. As we look around this "building" we notice that in this household, *Jesus* is the *chief cornerstone*, the *Hebrew* apostles and prophets are its *foundation* and we finish up with the completion of the Holy Temple of God being fit and built together *as His dwelling place* of God in the Spirit.

Does this remind you of God the Father's essential *question* in Isaiah 66:1–2, and of the *answer* to the Father's question found in John 14:23? The Father is seeking His house, His place of rest, and we, as human vessels are it. We are to dwell in the Son and the Father, and they in turn will make their abode in us as Their place of rest (John chapters 14–17).

Perhaps now you can understand why God wanted this book entitled "The Blueprint."

Since God's blueprint illustrates His dwelling place is to have Yeshua as its cornerstone and the Hebrew prophets and apostles as its foundation, perhaps we as Gentiles ought *to appreciate and honor* our Jewish foundational base to a much larger degree.

Brad Young in his work "Paul, the Jewish Theologian" spells out that Paul the Apostle described in Romans chapters 9 through 11 the Father's intent, through Yeshua, of *engrafting the Gentiles* as wild olive braches into the Hebrew root and fatness of the cultivated olive tree (Young 27–31). Per Young's explanation, Paul the Apostle taught that despite God's removal of some of the Hebrew branches based on their unbelief, God still did not cast His people away (Romans 11:1–5).

Paul lectured Gentiles not to become arrogant based on our new position as engrafted wild branches into the olive tree trunk since *remaining engrafted* is conditional.

*You will say then, "Branches were broken off that I might be grafted in." Well said. Because of unbelief they were broken off, and you stand by faith. **Do not be haughty**, but **fear**. For if God did not spare the natural branches, He may not spare you either. Therefore consider the goodness and severity of God: on those who fell, severity; but toward you, goodness, **if you continue** in His goodness. Otherwise you also will be cut off* (Romans11:19–22). (Emphasis added.)

Notice in the very next verse, we can see God's eventual plan *to again graft* into the olive tree *the original* cut-off branches (the Jews).

***And they also**, if they do **not** continue **in unbelief, will be grafted in, for God** is able to graft them **in again**. For if you were cut out of the olive tree which is wild by nature, and were grafted contrary to nature into a cultivated olive tree, how much more will these, **who are natural branches** be grafted into their own olive tree?* (Romans 11: 23–24) (Emphasis added.)

Is the grafting of the original branches back into the olive tree *a circular* process?

Was there a prototype example of what the "one new man" in Christ looked like back in the 1st century A.D.?

One example in the New Testament as to how Jesus the Messiah brought two distinct groups together as "one new man in Christ" to work together and share the Gospel with a world that did not know Christ can be seen in the 4th chapter of Paul's epistle to the Colossians. We see Paul as a prisoner recounting joint missionary events and receiving visitors from fellow disciples of Christ, both Jew and Gentile. Paul alludes to the various brethren by name while indicating that in spite of their differing ethnicities or cultural backgrounds, they are referred to as beloved brothers and comforting fellow workers. Two disparate groups—Jews and Gentiles—were dedicated to a common commitment to spread the Kingdom of God.

As the believing Hebrew fathers of the church were martyred, and the anchor of Jerusalem was crushed by Roman conquerors in 70 A.D., the Jews were dispersed, and the Christian message continued moving west. This geographical shifting along with the Jewish Diaspora beyond Israel's borders helped to create an intensification of the Hellenization of the Hebrew Gospel message. Negative writings against the Jews began to emerge more and more in the mid-second century, and anti-Jewish sentiment grew in the Empire after the Roman Emperor Constantine delivered an edict making Christianity the official religion of the Roman Empire. The ongoing ecclesiastical history of the Christian Church into the Middle Ages included several authors, theologians and officials who continued expanding the anti-Semitic message. During the later years of the Reformation, even Martin Luther himself attacked the Jews by writing about their "evil nature" while advocating for their penalization in a myriad of ways.

An example of the enduring harm of these early negative opinions of the Hebraic influence of the Bible emanates from an influential Church contributor Marcion of Sinope during the middle of the 2nd century. Marcion was all for pushing the idea that God had replaced the Jews. He "cherry picked" the Bible to form his own bible consisting of solely the Gospel of Luke and ten Pauline letters. He distorted the teachings of Paul despite claiming to be a follower. The Hebrew Testament was referred to as the "Old Testament", implying its obsolescence. The New Testament superseded the Old Covenant (The Hebrew Bible).

Marcion displayed deep roots of anti-Judaism and hatred of the Jewish people. His teachings included that Jewish testament law was negated in that the God of Israel (Yahweh) was actually the evil deity (Demiurge), the author of creation. He yearned for the higher, transcendent, true "god of light"—a god he believed had nothing to do with the God of Israel. He stood for the proposition that "The Father" to whom Jesus referred was a totally different God than the One who authored the creation of the earth (Young 33–36). According to Marcion, the teachings of Jesus bringing grace and compassion were incompatible with the "god" of the Old Testament who was a jealous, wrathful, ancestral god of the Jews who exacted retribution based on a legalistic foundation.

Although Marcion was eventually considered a heretic, his opinions spewing a disdain for Hebrew culture and religion *had an enduring impact* on some of the Church's approaches regarding the formation of a Canon of Christian Doctrine.

So today, despite our anti-Judaic, Christian Church history, what might this "one new man" in Christ look like now and into the future?

128

As author Brad Young points out, "Both Jesus, as the Anointed One of God, and Torah, occupy the position of centrality for the theology of the Apostle Paul. He is called to preach the message of Jesus the Messiah to the Gentile nations. Paul may indeed be described as a Pharisee, a Jewish theologian living among diverse groups of early Christians in the Greco-Roman world. *He was trying to bring the Jews and the non-Jews tightly together into the circle of early Christian community* through a more meaningful relationship one with the other, based on their common faith in God, the message of Jesus and the teachings contained within the Hebrew Bible" (Young 43).

In Galatians 3:28 Paul declared, "There is neither Jew nor Greek...for you are all one in Christ Jesus".

Young argued that while the apostle does not teach inequality, he recognizes ethnic and cultural distinctions and can rejoice in the differences. "The Gentile must not pretend to be Jewish by keeping all the ceremonial laws in the Torah. The Jewish believer must not behave like a Gentile, disregarding his or her rich heritage" (Young 137).

Paul the Apostle kept his Jewish identity amid the convergence of various groups of true believers (Galatians 5:3). Genuine camaraderie in Jesus brings about our ability to celebrate our distinctiveness as followers of Yeshua (Young 48).

I am a strong supporter of Gentiles using their assigned "keys to the Kingdom", having been enabled to unlock the "shut up words and sealed book" during these last days when many are running "to and fro" while knowledge is increasing (Daniel 12:4). We have much to learn about our God through our Jewish Biblical heritage. Let's acknowledge reality: without the Jew, there would be no Christian Church.

I contend that the Father wants to restore His messaging to us using the lenses of the Hebrew prophets and apostles. Although Messiah Yeshua (Jesus of Nazareth) has come and will come again, His fulfillment of Hebrew prophecy in so many contexts verifies the accuracy of the Hebrew Scripture in both testaments.

"Do not think that I came to destroy the Law or the Prophets. I did not come to destroy but to fulfill" (Matthew 5:17).

In my different teaching capacities, I have been given opportunities to teach a course entitled the "4 Great Types of Redemption". The word "types" in this context signifies symbols or shadows. God often communicates through symbols and shadows. The 4 types of redemption deal with the 7 Days of Creation, The Construction and Furnishings of the Tabernacle of Moses, the 7 Feasts of the Lord and the Journey from Egypt to Canaan. All four of these categories open up the God-inspired roadmaps that fulfill the Father's construction blueprint. Everything that occurs in this particular Hebrew typology study points to the Father's deliverance plan for mankind from rebellion through a Messiah, bringing us renewal and restoration of relationship with the Godhead. The goal is a *circular/cyclical* outline to redeem and restore God's errant children back to their Divine Father.

After learning the material as a student and later teaching the course as an instructor, I came away amazed at the majesty of our Father. As the Jews appreciate, He really is inscrutable and ineffable. His plan is a seamless one between two testaments and two very different people groups. And still, He is divinely able to supernaturally connect that which is seemingly not capable of being connected. Everything gets linked up, and the incongruous becomes coherent. It all begins to make sense. We are embarking on a *circular/cyclical journey* quite different from the Western, Greek, Platonic, Gnostic, *linear distortion* focusing on *relocation* as opposed to *reconciliation*. We have been sold a *linear* deviation from God's original *circular* redemption plan.

It is long past time to get back to our Hebrew roots so that we can better understand this God of Abraham, Isaac and Jacob who sent His Son as the Hebrew Messiah in the fulfillment of Hebrew Scripture and prophecies for the redemption of *all* mankind.

Our Role in Bringing About Restoration

Isn't it interesting that as we learn God's **goals for us as individuals**, it always comes back to learning and performing His perfect will? It was the *failure* to do His perfect will that brought death, disaster and devastation to mankind in the first place. The *only solution* to man's rebellion against God is to do His will.

Therefore, since Christ suffered for us in the flesh, **arm yourselves also with the same mind**, *for he who has suffered in the flesh has ceased from sin,* **that he no longer should live the rest of his time** *in the flesh for the lusts of men,* **but for the will of God** (1 Peter 4:1–2). (Emphasis added.)

There is a poignant bumper sticker I observed recently. It began and ended with a question: "Feel far away from God? Well, who moved?"

We have a central role in this restoration process. We have a *responsibility* to step into all that God the Father has made accessible to us through the victory of His Son's death on the cross and subsequent triumph over death.

*"Teacher, which is the great commandment in the law?" Jesus said to him, '**You shall love the Lord your God with all your***

heart with ***all*** your soul and with ***all*** your mind'. *"This is the first and great commandment"* (Matthew 22:36–38). (Emphasis added.)

A meaningful and significant relationship requires the participation of ***two*** individuals. *As of late, mankind doesn't seem to do relationship very well.* In our modern technological world, we are virtually tuned out. The enemy is well pleased with this. Distraction is his lethal game that he plays quite well. This game is ***lethal*** because the absence of the presence of God brings only death in the form of separation from God, not life.
If you don't believe Satan's tactics are lethal, try getting close to God and watch what happens to your thought life. The enemy will pull out all the stops in an attempt to flood your mind with minutia. Satan is well aware that once God's people become ***relationally reunited*** **with Him**, the Lord's original ***circular*** blueprint plan proves itself accurate. Thus, the three-way struggle for your love and attention in the pursuit of relationship begins and ends in your thought life.

For though we walk in the flesh, **we do not war according to the flesh**. *For the weapons of our warfare are not carnal but mighty in God for pulling down strongholds, casting down arguments and every high thing that exalts itself* **against the knowledge of God, bringing every thought into captivity to the obedience of Christ**...(2 Corinthians 10:3 5). (Emphasis added.)

The Battle is in the Mind

Throughout our jail ministry, we used to encourage the inmates to learn "obedience to Christ" though experiments with the intent of increasing their dialogue and relationship with the Godhead. We would conduct follow-up polls at the end of each week to determine the results of the experiments. We wanted to see whether the inmates had experienced any real change within their environments and within themselves.

For example, we would suggest that the inmates greet everyone they came in contact with *on their way* to breakfast in the cafeteria. However, during the 25-minute allotted mealtime, *they were not to say anything to anyone* unless directed to do so by the Holy Spirit. In essence, they were "plugging in" vertically to God and deciding to allow Him to run the show for 25 minutes.

Not surprisingly, the feedback during the follow-up polls was amazing. The inmates found that they generally spoke less during breakfast—*a lot less*. But when they did receive a directive to speak, what came out of their mouths *did not at all sound like* what would normally be expected of them. What would come forth were generally uplifting, encouraging, complimentary, positive and edifying words—shocking the messengers as much as the recipients.

The invaluable lesson the inmates were learning was what came out of their mouths was first formed in their minds. As they began to take "every thought captive unto the obedience of Christ" (2 Corinthians 10:5), they realized they were participating in a process *that brought the presence of God into their midst* and impacted the words that emanated from their mouths. This experiment resulted in palpable change in the atmosphere at that jail breakfast table. They were learning what "Thy will be done" actually looks like in real time, in their real world. The Kingdom of God had started to invade, permeate and change the jail setting—all because a few prisoners decided to implement "Thy will be done" during that present experimental moment.

Next, we upped the ante by having the inmates not say anything to anyone until instructed by the Holy Spirit at breakfast *as well as* during lunch *and* dinner. They were now communicating *directly* with God at all three mealtimes by plugging into Him vertically and requesting His presence. They later increased the frequency of "Kingdom invasions" to the outdoor exercise breaks of 30 minutes each day. Their frequency of contact with the Godhead began to take off, and by then, they were checking in with God at least four times a day.

When God's children begin to do His present-moment will, the impacts of His Kingdom cannot help but be noticed by others *outside* the family as well. The jail deputies began noticing the dramatic changes taking place within those four walls. The guards began asking us what we were teaching "in there" as they noticed that they were being treated with more respect. They also witnessed gangs dissolving and cross-racial Bible studies taking their place.

When sharing the gospel with inmates, I would always look for visual aids. One of the props I often used was a television remote control. I explained to the inmates that one of the buttons on the remote is a "pause" function that freeze-frames a moving image, allowing the picture to be studied more carefully in terms of its detail and content.

I explained that the same function applies in terms of bringing *every thought into captivity to the obedience of Christ.* Satan loves to rapidly introduce toxic, hurtful, rampaging thoughts into our minds, hoping that they will influence those of us running at high speed without a Holy Spirit "pause button".

However, once a thought is frozen in time, we can more closely study it by "plugging in vertically" to God and asking whether that particular thought originated with Him. If God's response is that *He did not send* the "freeze-framed" thought in question, then that only leaves two remaining sources for the thought's origin. Either the idea originated with us or it came from the enemy. Furthermore, if a thought does not produce one of the fruits of the Spirit—*love, joy, peace, patience, kindness, goodness, faithfulness, gentleness and self-control*—and instead brings mental torment, discouragement, anxiety, fear, anger, self-loathing, resentment, jealousy, envy, hopelessness, turmoil, unforgiveness, bitterness, self-pity or revenge, then in all likelihood it did not originate with either God or ourselves.

This elimination process now only leaves us with one alternative.

Satan is extremely skilled at making us believe that his suggestions are actually our own thoughts because of the personal pronoun "I" he inserts within each one:

- *I will probably never amount to anything, just like my father used to say to me.*

- *I'm a loser.*

- *I've always been like this.*

- *I can't do it.*

- *I will never forgive her for what she said.*

- *I have the right not to forgive him because I was a victim.*

- *I know things never work out for my benefit.*

- *Why should I even bother?*

- *I don't think they want to be with me anyway.*

- *I will never measure up to them.*

- *I know they're all against me.*

- *I don't have time for emotions.*

- *I'm worthless.*

- *I won't ever let anyone hurt me again.*

- *I don't accept limits; they fence me in.*

- *I'm the captain of my ship.*

- *I don't think it will ever be my turn.*

Do any of these thoughts produce the Holy Spirit fruits of *love, joy, peace, patience, kindness, goodness, faithfulness, gentleness or self-control*? Do any of them line up with your divine family identity, consistent with your ranking as a child of the Most High God? Do any of them bring you closer into the presence of God?

Or do the above-listed thoughts comport more with Satan's poisonous lies denigrating your image and identity as a member of God's royal family?

We challenged the inmates to align their thoughts with the truth and accuracy of what the word of God said about them. We reminded them that as followers of Christ, they are not only *children* of God but also *heirs as members of His family*. (See below Romans 8:15-17). We advised them that God's word says that we are all fearfully and wonderfully made (Psalm 139:14), and God has fashioned our days for us.

These truths of God regarding their value and divine family status began to set them free from the bondage of Satan's lies of warped identity and hopelessness.

"And you shall know the truth, and the truth shall make you free" (John 8:32).

For you did not receive the spirit of bondage again to fear, but you received the Spirit of adoption by whom we cry out, "Abba, Father." The Spirit Himself bears witness with our spirit that we are children of God, and if children, then heirs, heirs of God and joint heirs with Christ if indeed we suffer with him, that we may also be glorified together. (Romans 8:15–17)

The inmates were beginning to believe and actually partake in the **restoration process**, fulfilling God's **goals of union and rest** with Him. They were becoming transformed into the **image** of God's Son, Jesus Christ.

*And what agreement has the temple of God with idols? For you are the temple of the living God. As God has said: "**I will dwell in them** and walk among them. **I will be their God, and they shall be My people.**" Therefore, "Come out from among them and be separate says the Lord. Do not touch what is unclean, and I will receive you." "**I will be a Father to you, and you shall be My sons and daughters says the Lord Almighty**"* (2 Corinthians 6:16–18). (Emphasis added.)

*But we all, with unveiled face beholding as in a mirror the glory of the Lord, **are being transformed into the same image from glory to glory**, just as by the Spirit of the Lord* (2 Corinthians 3:18). (Emphasis added.)

In addition to God's goal of completing a *full circle experience* to **relationally restore** His blueprint, that same blueprint also includes **restoring God's original roles for man as priests and**

rulers. We are to be responsible for dominion over the earth under the headship of Christ. In the context of God's original blueprint, how does one qualify for future Kingdom roles? There is a Kingdom principle that to whom much is given much is required. In many of the parables of Jesus, there is a recurrent theme of how stewards were either rewarded or punished based on their faithfulness with that which they were entrusted. We as Christians have been afforded much: the cross, the precious blood of the Lamb and the Holy Spirit—all designed to draw us back to our Father. That which we have received is not intended solely for our benefit. We are to be God's witnesses, representatives and agents, ***bringing life to others*** so that the ***world may know*** that the Father sent His Son to redeem His creation.

*"I in them, and You in Me; that they may be made perfect in one, and **that the world may know** that You have sent Me, and have loved them as You have loved Me"* (John 17:23). (Emphasis added.)

*On the last day, that great day of the feast, Jesus stood and cried out, saying, "If anyone thirsts, let him come to Me and drink. "He who believes in Me as the Scripture has said, **out of his heart** will **flow rivers of living water**"* (John 7:37-38). (Emphasis added.)

For everyone to whom much is given, from him much will be required; and to whom much has been committed, of him they will ask the more (Luke 12:48b).

We as Christians will begin to realize that the free will decisions we actively make in real time have both present and everlasting consequences. We will also begin to realize that God directs our earthly experiences that are designed for our Kingdom roles' training and growth.

138

*And from Jesus Christ, the faithful witness, the first born from the dead, and the ruler over the kings of the earth. To Him who loved us and washed us from our sins in His own blood, **and has made us kings and priests to His God and Father**, to Him be glory and dominion forever and ever. Amen* (Revelation 1:5–6). (Emphasis added.)

We informed the inmates that due to being granted such tremendous responsibility and opportunity, we all will be required to give a face-to-face account to Jesus Christ, to whom our heavenly Father has afforded all judgment, on how we lived our lives and how well we carried out His will.

*For the Father judges no one, **but has committed all judgment to the Son**, "For as the Father has life in Himself, so He has granted the Son to have life in Himself, **and has given Him authority to execute judgment also, because he is the Son of Man*** (John 5:22, 26–27). (Emphasis added.)

*Therefore we make it our aim, whether present or absent, to be well pleasing to Him. For **we must all** appear before **the judgment seat of Christ**, that **each one** may **receive the things done in the body, according to what he has done**, whether good or bad. Knowing, therefore, the terror of the Lord, we persuade men...* (2 Corinthians 5:9–11a). (Emphasis added.)

While speaking with a recent Christian convert, he wondered that since we are not saved by our works, how then is it possible that we will be judged by them? I explained to him that a critical difference exists between dead religious works involving rituals, dietary requirements and circumcision contrasted with responsive, loving, obedient works flowing from a dynamic, personal relationship with the Godhead. My friend was surprised to learn that Jesus said that He did not come to do away with the Law, but rather to fulfill it.

"Do not think that I came to destroy the Law or the Prophets. I did not come to destroy but to fulfill. For assuredly, I say to you, till heaven and earth pass away, one jot or one tittle will by no means pass from the law till all is fulfilled. Whoever therefore breaks one of the least of these commandments, and teaches men so, shall be called least in the kingdom of heaven; but whoever does and teaches them, he shall be called great in the kingdom of heaven. For I say to you, that unless your righteousness exceeds the righteousness of the scribes and Pharisees, you will by no means enter the kingdom of heaven" (Matthew 5:17–20).

If you encounter a similar situation, you may want to ask the individual what the difference is between a gift and a prize. A gift is simply received, while a prize is striven for, earned and won.

"He who overcomes shall inherit all things, and I will be his God and he shall be My son" (Revelation 21:7).

We taught the inmates that as Christians, we are always under some kind of law. Through Messiah's death on the cross, it is true that we are no longer under the Mosaic Law of sacrifices, rituals, observances and requirements. However, when Paul said we are no longer under the Law, he never pronounced doing away with **the *moral requirements*** of the original Law of Moses. Rather, as blood-washed Christians, we are subject to the new "Law of the Spirit of Life in Christ Jesus" (Romans 8:2), which is actually an *expansion* of the moral requirements under the Law of Moses.

*There is therefore now no condemnation to those who are in Christ Jesus, who do not **walk** according to the flesh, but **according to the Spirit**. **For the law of the Spirit of life in Christ Jesus** has made me free from the law of sin and death* (Romans 8:1–2).

For example, when Jesus explained that if one were to so much as look at a woman with lust, that person had already committed adultery with her. Jesus' teaching here was actually **an** *expansion* of the Law of Moses, which only forbade the actual act of adultery. In another example, we see Jesus again *expanding* the requirements of Mosaic Law when He addressed the rich young ruler that he was to sell all and to follow Him. Jesus added these requirements after the rich young ruler had earlier boasted that he had kept all of the moral requirements of the Mosaic Law. But Jesus knew the heart of the issue and He knew the heart of the rich, young ruler. *The expansion and personal application of the law of the Spirit of life in Christ Jesus* revealed the true motivations of the ruler, and the ruler went away saddened that he was unwilling to sell all that was so important to him.

My recently converted friend also assumed that due to current church teachings, *the main emphasis of the new covenant* is one of forgiveness only—distinct from the sin and judgment of the old covenant. However, he was unaware that *forgiveness of sin already previously existed under the Mosaic covenant through animal sacrifices*, and the *main emphasis of the new covenant* involves **the powerful divine change of us** from the inside out. This internal divine change of us occurs as the Lord, through the Holy Spirit, places His laws into our hearts and writes His laws in our minds. *The new covenant ultimately brings about our being liberated from the power of Satan and the compulsion to continue sinning. This happens through the Holy Spirit empowering us to fall in love with God and demonstrate our love to Him by obeying His commands.*

But this Man, after He had offered one sacrifice for sins forever, sat down at the right hand of God, from that time waiting till His enemies are made His footstool. For by one offering He has perfected forever those **who are being sanctified**. *But the Holy Spirit also witnesses to us; for after*

*He had said before, **"This is the covenant that I will make with them after those days**, says the Lord: **I will put My laws into their hearts and in their minds I will write them,"** then He adds, "Their sins and their lawless deeds I will remember no more"* (Hebrews 10:12–17). (Emphasis added.)

*I say then: **Walk in the Spirit**, and you shall **not** fulfill **the lust of the flesh*** (Galatians 5:16). (Emphasis added.)

*Therefore, having these promises, beloved, **let us cleanse ourselves** from all filthiness of the flesh and spirit**, perfecting holiness in the fear of God*** (2 Corinthians 7:1). (Emphasis added.)

*And those who are Christ's have crucified the flesh with its passions and desires. **If we live in the Spirit, let us also walk in the Spirit*** (Galatians 5:24–25).

*If indeed you have heard Him and have been taught by Him, as the truth is in Jesus: **that you put off** concerning your former conduct, **the old man** which grows corrupt according to the deceitful lust, **and be renewed in the spirit of your mind**, **and that you put on the new man** which was created according to God in true righteousness and holiness* (Ephesians 4: 21–24). (Emphasis added.)

Forgiveness of sin in the new covenant is not its main message. The essence of the new covenant *is change*. It is a changing of us from the image and power of Satan to the image and power of Christ by and through the empowerment of the Holy Spirit. Lasting change occurs when we allow the presence of God to become so active in our lives that we begin to obey the Lord naturally by the power of the Holy Spirit.

*'...to open their eyes in order **to turn them** from darkness to light, and **from the power of Satan to God**, that they may receive forgiveness of sins and an inheritance among those who are sanctified by faith in Me'* (Acts 26:18). (Emphasis added.)

*And do not be conformed to this world, but **be transformed by the renewing of your mind, that you may prove what is that good and acceptable and perfect will of God*** (Romans 12:2). (Emphasis added.)

But let a man examine himself, and so let him eat of the bread and drink of the cup. For if we would judge ourselves, we would not be judged. But when we are judged, we are chastened by the Lord that we may not be condemned with the world (1 Corinthians 11:28, 31–32).

This change also transpires by means of a *restorative process* consisting of personal encounters with God to build our faith in the character and the qualities of our Father. Continual testing takes place as a normal occurrence of our maturation process. The Father has to know and be satisfied with the depth and quality of our relationship with Him. He has to know whether we will continue to carry out His will, come what may. Just as the Jews were to learn in the desert to follow the cloud by day and the pillar of fire by night, we are to be led and guided by the Holy Spirit in everything we think, say and do. This does not occur overnight. Look at the Old Testament symbolism here: After God **saves/redeems us** from the angel of death at Passover, He leads us out of Egypt into our own personal "Sinai desert" so that we can learn His ways and begin to depend on Him for everything so that we may live. He is **restoring** us to a **full circle return** to pure relationship with Him.

It is the Holy Spirit who provides the power to overcome our rebellious compulsion to continue sinning. In the jail setting, we instructed the inmates what it looks like to be led by the Spirit.

*For if you live according to the flesh you will die; but if **by the Spirit** you put to death the deeds of the body, **you will live*** (Romans 8:13). (Emphasis added.)

We taught them how to live in the present tense. It is something I call the "two-second drill": You have no control over your past other than to learn from it. You have no control over your future other than allowing God to run it. What you do have control over is your present moment reality. The question becomes to whom will you give your thought life for the next two seconds? It is a free will decision for which we are responsible. Our present-time decisions have consequences both in the spiritual world and in the material world. Controlling your thought life for two-second increments, impacts the words that come out of your mouth. This two-second thought drill begins to change you into the image of Christ. The more you practice turning over your immediate thought life to God two seconds at a time, the easier it becomes.

*For though we walk in the flesh, we do not war according to the flesh. **For the weapons of our warfare are not carnal but mighty in God** for pulling down strongholds, casting down arguments and every high thing that exalts itself against the knowledge of God, **bringing every thought into captivity to the obedience of Christ*** (2 Corinthians 10:3–5). (Emphasis added.)

*Therefore, brethren, we are debtors-not to the flesh, to live according to the flesh. For if you live according to the flesh you will die; **but if by the Spirit you put to death the deeds of the body, you will live. For as many as are led by the Spirit of***

God, these are sons of God (Romans 8:12–14). (Emphasis added.)

As you allow yourself to be led by the Holy Spirit you need to begin living a "two-second thought life". You start to become a child of God and a coheir with Christ by coming into union with the Father, the Son and the Holy Spirit, who over time produce your change into Their image.

But we all, with unveiled face, beholding as in a mirror the glory of the Lord, **are being transformed into the same image** *from glory to glory just* **as by the Spirit of the Lord** (2 Corinthians 3:18). (Emphasis added.)

The Kingdom of God invaded the dark walls of our local jails. We actually witnessed Satan's government being dispossessed and replaced. The Gospel account was coming *full circle*. The Father's blueprint was being *restored*. The inmates experienced *restoration* back to the Father. We too, as we cooperate, are eligible for the same *circular* blessing.

Chapter 8

Why is there "Power in the Blood"?

According to Webster's Dictionary, one of the synonyms listed for *"power"* is the word *"authority"*, which implies the granting of power for a specific purpose within specified limits. Another synonym, *"jurisdiction"*, applies to official power exercised within the prescribed limits of *"authority"*. The word *"control"* stresses the power to direct and restrain, and *"command"* implies the power to make decisions and compel obedience. (*Merriam-Webster.com*, Merriam-Webster, 2015. Web. 11 November 2015).

When recently asked to preach at a local church, I was impressed upon by the Lord to ask a question of the congregation. First, I asked them if they were familiar with the old hymn "Power in the Blood". Most had heard of the song, either from their current churches or from childhood memories. The chorus repeats that there is "power, power, wonder working power in the blood of the Lamb." My next question to the congregation was "Have you ever asked yourself *why* there is power in the blood of the lamb?" Aside from the expected answers of saving us from hell and allowing us to go to Heaven, no one really answered the question.

The true answer as to *why* there is so much power in the blood lies in understanding *why* the Father sent His Son, Jesus Christ. Jesus came to die for our sins so that we, too, can die to sin and live for righteousness (1 Peter 2:24).

Christ will destroy the works of the devil (1 John 3:8) and redeem us from every lawless deed so that we restore our relationship with the Father and the Son by obeying their commandments, through which we will inherit eternal life (John 14:21,23 and John 17:3). In other words, we must live out "Thy will be done" as commanded of us in the Lord's Prayer. It must become our lifestyle and lifeblood, just as it was for Jesus.

*Jesus said to them, "**My food is to do the will of Him who sent Me**, and to finish His work* (John 4:34). (Emphasis added.)

*I can of Myself do nothing. As I hear, I judge; and My judgment is righteous, **because I do not seek My own will but the will of the Father Who sent Me*** (John 5:30). (Emphasis added.)

*Though He was a Son, **yet He learned obedience** by the things which He suffered. And having been perfected, He became the author of eternal salvation **to all who obey Him*** (Hebrews 5:8–9). (Emphasis added.)

Throughout His ministry, Jesus had several opportunities to follow His Father's will, which were often followed by signs and wonders in the form of miracles. ***Obedience comes first, then genuine divine power follows***. In order for there to be a manifestation of ***genuine*** divine power, there must first be total submission to God's will through obeying His directives down to the smallest detail.

Examples of this principle can be observed all throughout Jesus' ministry on earth. Look how Christ's obedience provided direct access for mankind *back to our Father*.

*Previously saying, "Sacrifice and offering, burnt offerings, and offerings for sin You did not desire, nor had pleasure in them" (which are offered according to the law), **then He said, "Behold I have come to do your will, oh God"*** (obedience-produced cause). *He takes away the first that He may establish* *the second.* **By that will we have been sanctified through the offering of the body of Jesus Christ once for all.** (obedience-produced cause). *And every priest stands ministering daily and offering repeatedly the same sacrifices, which can never take away sins.* **But this Man, after He had offered one sacrifice for sins forever,** (obedience-produced cause) **sat down at the right hand of God,** (effect-divine power) *from that time waiting till His enemies are made His footstool. For by one offering* **He has perfected forever those who are being sanctified** (effect-divine power). *But the Holy Spirit also witnesses to us; for after He had said before,* **"This is the covenant that I will make with them after those days, says the Lord: I will put My laws into their hearts, and in their minds I will write them,"** (effect–divine power). *Then He adds,* "Their sins and their lawless deeds I will remember no more." *Now where there is remission of these, there is no longer an offering for sin.* **Therefore, brethren, having boldness to enter the Holiest by the blood of Jesus,** (effect – divine power) *By a new and living way* **which He consecrated for us, through the veil, that is, His flesh,** (effect-divine power) *And having a High Priest over the house of God,* **Let us draw near** (effect-divine power) *with a true heart in full assurance of faith, having our hearts sprinkled from an evil conscience and our bodies washed with pure water* (Hebrews 10:8–22). (Emphasis and key words added.)

And Jesus cried out again with a loud voice, **and yielded up His spirit,** (obedience produced cause). *Then, behold,* **the veil of the temple was torn in two from top to bottom** *and the earth quaked and the rocks were split, and the graves were opened;* **and many bodies of the saints who had fallen asleep were raised;** (effect–divine power) *and coming out of the graves after His resurrection* **they went into the holy city and appeared to many** (Matthew 27:50–53). (Emphasis and key words added.)

*Jesus said to him, "I am the way, the truth, and the life. No one comes **to the Father except through Me*** (John 14:6). (Emphasis added.)

*And Jesus came and spoke to them, saying, "All authority has been given to Me in heaven and on earth. Assuredly, I say to you whatever you bind on earth will be bound in heaven, and whatever you loose on earth will be loosed in heaven. Again I say to you that **if two of you agree on earth concerning anything that they ask**,* (obedience produced cause) ***it will be done for them by My Father in heaven"*** (effect–divine power) (Matthew 18:18–19). (Emphasis and key words added.)

"*Most assuredly, I say to you, **he who believes in Me*** (obedience produced cause), ***the works that I do he will do also; and greater works than these he will do,*** (effect–divine power) *because I go to My Father"* (John 14:12). (Emphasis and the key words added.)

So in that moment of trial in the Garden of Gethsemane, with that singular decision made by Jesus our Lord and Savior to obey our Father's will, the Father's plan for the *remainder* of His children became attainable. The power flowing from Jesus' decision to obey our Father to offer up His life up on the cross, ***changed the course of history forever***. Mankind from that point forward was able to come boldly before the Father's throne through the veil of the Son's flesh.

*Though He was a Son, **yet He learned obedience** by the things which He suffered* (obedience-produced cause). *And having been perfected, **He became the author of eternal salvation** to all who obey Him* (effect-divine power) (Hebrews 5:8–9). (Emphasis and key words added.)

For we do not have a High Priest who cannot sympathize with our weaknesses, but was in all points tempted as we are, yet without sin (obedience-produced cause). ***Let us therefore come boldly to the throne of grace****, that we may obtain mercy and find grace to help in time of need* (effect-divine power) (Hebrews 4:15–16). (Emphasis and key words added.)

As a result of the **obedient sacrifice** of Jesus, mankind *once again* had access to a Father-child relationship as adopted children (completing God's blueprint circle), along with all of the rights, title and interest of full-fledged members of the royal family.

For you did not receive the spirit of bondage again to fear, ***but you received the Spirit of adoption by whom we cry out "Abba, Father."*** *The Spirit himself bears witness with our spirit* ***that we are children of God, and if children, then heirs—heirs of God and joint heirs with Christ,*** *if we indeed suffer with Him, that we may also be glorified together* (Romans 8: 15–17). (Emphasis added.)

Talk about miraculous power *following* obedience!

If Jesus, as God's Son, had to learn obedience, how much more then, is required of us? The same strategic implementation of God's will can happen in our own spheres of influence, whether within our neighborhoods, workplaces or under our own roofs with our families. *As long as we obey* the direction of the Lord through the Holy Spirit, there is no limit to His subsequent release of divine power through us.

What Power in the Blood Means for Us

When Jesus commenced His ministry, His message was a continuation of John the Baptist's, which was essentially that mankind should *repent* because the *"kingdom of heaven"* was at hand. A governmental replacement over the earth and its people was about to occur. The **dominion** over the **domain** of earth was about to change. Christ's announcement signaled that the days of Satan's kingdom of rebellion over the earth were numbered. The sovereignty over God's creation of earth and mankind would no longer be in question. God's plan *to restore* His *original* blueprint of mankind gaining eternal life through *relationship* with the Father and *rulership* over the earthly creation had been launched through Jesus' physical arrival on the earth.

*For unto us a Child is born, unto us a Son is given; and the **government** will be upon His shoulder. And His name will be called Wonderful, Counselor, Mighty God, Everlasting Father, Prince of Peace. Of the increase of **His government** and peace there will be no end, Upon the throne of David and over **His Kingdom, To order it and establish it with judgment and justice from that time forward, even forever.** The zeal of the Lord of hosts will perform this* (Isaiah 9:6–7). (Emphasis added.)

When we realize that the Gospel message is really a promise and a plan of substituting one government for another, it brings another **circular** perspective to the whole story. As such, **the circular end game** is not being sent to Heaven but rather that God's Kingdom is being sent from Heaven down to earth.

This **circular** Kingdom message changes everything. It changes perspective. It changes people. It changes goals. It changes roles. It changes destiny.

Kings, not democratically elected representatives, run kingdoms. Jesus Christ of Nazareth is the King of kings and Lord of lords.

Then the seventh angel sounded: and there were loud voices in heaven, saying, "The kingdoms of this world have become the kingdoms of our Lord and of His Christ, and He shall reign forever and ever!" (Revelation 11:15).

The Kingdom of God belongs to Yeshua and correspondingly, belongs to us as well.

*"I will declare the decree: the Lord has said to Me, '**You are My Son**, Today I have begotten You. **Ask of Me, and I will give you the nations for Your inheritance, and the ends of the earth for Your possession**. You shall break them with a rod of iron; You shall dash them to pieces like a potters vessel'"* (Psalms 2:7–9). (Emphasis added.)

*And Jesus came and spoke to them, saying, "**All authority** has been given **to Me** in heaven and on earth* (Matthew 28:18). (Emphasis added.)

*The Spirit Himself bears witness with our spirit that we are children of God, and if children, then heirs – heirs of God **and joint heirs with Christ**, if indeed we suffer with Him that we may also be glorified together* (Romans 8:16–17). (Emphasis added.)

*"**To him who overcomes I will grant to sit with Me on My throne**, as I also overcame and sat down with My Father on His throne* (Revelation 3:21). (Emphasis added.)

Christ also delegated to us His same authority and power *over* the enemy.

*"Go therefore and make disciples of all nations, **baptizing them** in the name of the Father and of the Son **and of the Holy Spirit, teaching them to observe all things I have commanded you**; and lo, I am with you always, even to the end of the age"* (Matthew 28:19–20). (Emphasis added.)

And He said to them, "Go into all the world and preach the gospel to every creature. "He who believes and is baptized will be saved; but he who does not believe will be condemned. "And these signs will follow those who believe: In My name they will have cast out demons; they will speak with new tongues; "they will take up serpents; and if they drink anything deadly, it will by no means hurt them; they will lay hands on the sick, and they will recover."(Mark 16:15–18).

*"But **you shall receive power when the Holy Spirit** has come upon you; **and you shall be witnesses to Me** in Jerusalem, and in all Judea and Samaria, and to the end of the earth"* (Acts 1:8). (Emphasis added.)

The result is that we no longer have to serve rebellion and disobedience (Romans 6). ***Through access to the Holy Spirit, we now have the authority and power over all sin against God.*** All we have to do is choose to appropriate Christ's victory on the cross and His reestablishment of God's Kingdom over the earth and internally within ourselves. We are finally *free* from the compulsion to disobey God. We are at last liberated.

*But **if the Spirit of Him** who raised Jesus from the dead **dwells in you**, He who raised Christ from the dead will also give life to your mortal bodies through His Spirit who dwells in you. Therefore, brethren, we are debtors—not to the flesh, to live according to the flesh. For if you live according to the flesh you will die; **but if by the Spirit** you put to death the deeds of the body, you will live. **For as many as are led by the Spirit of God**, these are sons of God* (Romans 8:11–14). (Emphasis added.)

We Are Led By the Spirit

Our challenge is to learn ***how to be led*** by the Spirit of God.

154

What in the world does that look like?

God's divine power flows to us and through us as we start to finally obey His commandments, beginning with transitioning from an uncontrolled, rampaging thought life to one of focusing on Him.

*For though we walk in the flesh, we do not war according to the flesh. For the weapons of our warfare are not carnal but mighty in God for pulling down strongholds, casting down arguments and every high thing that exalts itself against the knowledge of God, **bringing every thought into captivity to the obedience of Christ** (2 Corinthians 10:3-5). (Emphasis added.)*

The *dedication* and *love* of Jesus *for* our Heavenly Father, **which was demonstrated by His obeying the Father's will to the point of death**, explains *why* "there is power in the blood". **At the moment Jesus decided** to go to the cross **in obedience** to His Father's will, **Satan lost all access and influence of power over Christ**.

In turn, **Satan loses** access and influence of power **over us** when we begin to decide, even if it costs us our very lives, **to obey** our Heavenly Father's will.

Obeying the Father's will to the point of death is **why** there is "*power in the blood.*" **Loving obedience trumps rebellion every time.** Obedience is the measuring rod of the depth and quality of our relationship with the Most High God.

*"**And they overcame him** by the blood of the Lamb and **by** the word of their testimony, **and they did not love their lives to the death** (Revelation 12:11). (Emphasis added.)*

As the Lord gets His way with us, ("Thy will be done"), the world begins to see Him living inside us as human houses of

God. The world begins to see the qualities of Christ through our words, our actions and our motives!

*"I in them, and You in Me; that they may be made perfect in one, and **that the world may know** that You have sent Me, and have loved them as You have loved Me* (John 17:23). (Emphasis added.)

Doing "Thy will be done" ushers in the Kingdom of God into the present moment. We actually begin to be the salt and light and begin to do some earthly good in the here and now instead of focusing solely on the future. If we take care of the present moment, the future will take care of itself. If we can just learn to listen to the Lord through the Holy Spirit, we will discover what He wants us to think now, what to say now and what to do now.

*Beloved, now we are children of God; and it has not yet been revealed what we shall be, but we know that when He is revealed, **we shall be like Him** (image), for we shall see Him as He is. And everyone who has this hope in Him purifies himself (obedience), just as He is pure. **Whoever abides in Him** (union) **does not sin**. Whoever sins has neither seen him nor knows Him. He who sins is of the devil, for the devil has sinned from the beginning. For this purpose the Son of God was manifested, that He might destroy (kingdom vs. kingdom) the works of the devil* (I John 3:2–3, 6, 8). (Emphasis and parenthetical words added.)

I submit that God's word teaches us that we were first saved *in order to learn how to fall in love with God **and to demonstrate our love by obeying Him** in all our affairs.* As we do, God's goals that we become more like Him and become one with Him begin to become reality. We begin to become *actual witnesses* of and for the Lord.

*"If you **love** me, **keep** my commandments* (John 14:15). (Emphasis added.)

*"**But you shall receive power** when the Holy Spirit has come upon you; **and you shall be witnesses to me**...and to the end of the earth"* (Acts 1:8). (Emphasis added.)

Divine power *follows* Kingdom obedience, which brings glory to God and His government. **There is *power in the blood* because *Jesus obeyed* the *will of our Father to the point of death*** so that we would have life and have it abundantly.

For Yours is the kingdom and the power and the glory forever. Amen (Matthew 6:13b).

Chapter 9

Caveat Credens
(Let the Believer Beware)

In commercial law, there is a Latin phrase that acts as a warning for consumers: "Caveat emptor", which means: "Let the buyer beware". There appears to be a contemporary corresponding spiritual warning for Christian and Messianic Jewish believers: "Let the believer beware."

With the rapid acceleration of current world events, *we see God sending us signs and signals.* In 2014 and 2015 alone, along with early 2016 financial warnings, we have witnessed the beginning of the Hebrew feast calendar fulfillment of the *Shemitah* season (Leviticus 25) along with heavenly signs of the tetrad consisting of four *blood moons* (four complete lunar eclipses) that have fallen for two years on the exact *Hebrew festivals* of Passover and Tabernacles.

*Then God said, **"Let there be lights** in the firmament **of the heavens** to divide the day from the night; **and let them be for signs and seasons** and for days and years; Then God made two great lights: the greater light to rule the day, and the lesser light to rule the night. He made the stars also* (Genesis 1:14,16). (Emphasis added.)

A more in-depth study of Shemitah is beyond the scope of this book but is well worth obtaining the additional information regarding *the fulfillment of God's time clock through prophecy, signs and signals in the heavens and the Shemitah Sabbath*. I would draw your attention to two books by Messianic Rabbi Jonathan Cahn entitled "The Harbinger" and

"The Mystery of the Shemitah" as well as the book "Blood Moons" by Pastor Mark Biltz.

Satan Still Wants to Run the Show

Whether through outside influence, unscriptural teachings, internal access or actual possession, Satan has always wanted to take over God's plan for mankind on the earth (Isaiah 14 and Ezekiel 28). As the great deceiver, he obtains his power over the saints by getting us to believe in his lies that twist, distort, pervert and ultimately deviate us from God's will.

*Now the Spirit expressly says that **in latter times** some will depart from the faith, **giving heed to deceiving spirits** and doctrines of demons, speaking lies in hypocrisy having their own conscience seared with a hot iron* (1 Timothy 4:1–2). (Emphasis added.)

For the time will come when they will not endure sound doctrine, but according to their own desires, because they have itching ears, they will heap up for themselves teachers; and they will turn their ears away from the truth and be turned aside to fables (2 Timothy 4:3–4).

"You are of your father the devil, and the desires of your father you want to do. He was a murderer from the beginning, and does not stand in the truth, because there is no truth in him. When he speaks a lie, he speaks from his own resources, for he is a liar and the father of it (John 8:44).

And no wonder! For Satan himself transforms himself into an angel of light (2 Corinthians 11:14).

Satan doesn't waste any time or attention on the "lost", as he has already duped them. Rather, he focuses on the saints attempting to pursue God's goals. He tends to hang around churches and gathering places of believers. His task is to study and to detour God's church by implanting confusion, discord and turmoil and does so through stealth, imitation, and subterfuge. And time and again he has shown he is really good at what he does.

For example, in Matthew 7:21–23, there was a group of believers who were seemingly operating in the signs and wonders of the Kingdom of God using powerful signs, wonders and giftings. There was only one problem: Not one aspect of the Godhead was involved in their demonstrations. Jesus stated that despite their claiming "Lord, Lord", they failed to enter into the Kingdom of Heaven because they were not carrying out the will of the Father. Despite their claims to have prophesied, cast out demons and performed wonders in the Lord's name, Jesus declared He never knew them. *Adding insult to injury, He labeled them as lawless* and commanded them to depart from Him.

*"Not everyone who says to Me, 'Lord, Lord', shall enter the kingdom of heaven, but he who does the will of My Father in heaven". **Many** will say to Me in that day, ' Lord, Lord, have we not prophesied in Your name, cast out demons in Your name, and done many wonders in Your name?' "And then I will declare to them, 'I never knew you; depart from Me you who practice lawlessness!'* (Matthew 7:21–23). (Emphasis added.)

Something had gone terribly wrong. How could the assumptions of these apparently gifted "believers" have been so off the mark? The only explanation is that these apparent "heavy hitters" *had been successfully deceived.*

In Matthew 24:26, Jesus answered a question posed by his disciples regarding the sign of His coming at the end of the age. One of the signs that Jesus mentioned leading up to His return involves the rise of many false prophets who will *deceive* many during this period of tribulation. He later went on to mention that ***false christs and false prophets will rise and show great signs and wonders to deceive, if possible, even the elect***!

So how was it possible that these "heavy hitters" had been successfully deceived? I am convinced that the answer to this question lies in Matthew 7:23. After Jesus refused to be impressed by all the claims of signs and wonders, prophecies and demonic deliverances by these presumptuous performers, Jesus declared ***that He never knew those same practitioners who exercised lawlessness.*** The reason Jesus claimed He did not know those doing great signs and wonders in His name was because they were ***practicing lawlessness***—they were disobedient. He warned that *many* would be called lawless and would suffer the ultimate fate of having to depart from the Lord. Due to their failure to establish what God wanted in their circumstances, their works revealed that they did not even *know* Christ. If they had known Him, they would have verified the will of the Lord for the issue at hand. In turn, they would have verified the will of the Father.

*Jesus said to them,"My food **is to do the will of Him** who sent Me, and to finish His work"* (John 4:34). (Emphasis added.)

*"My sheep **hear My voice**, and **I know** them, and **they follow Me*** (John 10:27). (Emphasis added.)

*"Do you not believe that I am in the Father, and the Father in Me? The words that I speak to you **I do not speak on my own authority; but the Father who dwells in Me does the works**. Believe me that I am in the Father and the Father in Me, or else believe Me for the sake of the works themselves"* (John 14:10–11). (Emphasis added.)

162

though He was a Son, yet He learned obedience by the things which He suffered. And having been perfected, **He became the author of eternal salvation to all who obey Him,** ... (Hebrews 5:8–9). (Emphasis added.)

How can we as Christ followers know what His will is in a particular circumstance? If we are asking, listening and conversing with God the Father or His Son Jesus, then those are good indications that we indeed "know" Him. And if we "know" Him, then we should be able to discern His will in most circumstances. If we are able to discern His will, then we should be able to carry out the instructions included in His will. The Bible weighs in on this issue relative to how we are able to prove what God's will is in a particular matter.

"I beseech you therefore, brethren, by the mercies of God, that you present your bodies a living sacrifice, holy, acceptable to God, which is your reasonable service. And do not be conformed to this world, **but be transformed by the renewing of your mind,** *that you* **may prove** *what is that good and acceptable and perfect* **will** *of God"* (Romans 12:1–2). (Emphasis added.)

In the end times, as false christs and false prophets will start to rise with displays of great signs and wonders meant to deceive all—even the elect—*the only way* to discern between genuine divine power and false imitations will be to verify whether the signs and wonders are based on *obedience to God.* We as saints need to avail ourselves of the *gift of discerning of spirits* from the Holy Spirit (1 Corinthians 12:10). Learning how to discern the voice of the Lord is tricky business. It takes a lot of practice.

So, exactly *how* do we renew our minds so that we may prove the perfect will of God as specified in Romans 12:1-2 cited above? Again the Bible weighs in with the perfect instructional responses.

*"For though we walk in the flesh, we do not war according to the flesh. For the weapons of our warfare are not carnal but mighty in God for pulling down strongholds, casting down arguments and every high thing that exalts itself against the knowledge of God, **bringing every thought into captivity to the obedience of Christ**"* (2 Corinthians 10:3–5).

***Now by this we know that we know Him, if we keep His commandments**. He who says, "I know Him," and does not keep His Commandments, is a liar, and the truth is not in him* (1 John 2:3–4). (Emphasis added.)

***We are to hold up our every thought to the mirror of obeying Christ. Obedience to God is the linchpin to everything**.* It is the measuring rod of whether we truly know Christ and whether "end times" signs and wonders are the "real deal" or are nothing more than counterfeit depictions. Understanding this divine reality will ultimately result in either union or separation from Jesus.

"If you love Me, keep My Commandments" (John 14:15).

We also must shy away from "fast moving vehicles" (like the "latest" or "most popular" church trends or programs) that seek out bogus hype/glitz of imitation Holy Spirit movements without obedience to the Father. The *core* of any *genuine* Holy Spirit movement must always be centered around the concept of "Thy will be done". To simply pursue "the fireworks" leaves us vulnerable to be victimized, as Jesus had prophesied warning us about deceptive end times environments.

*"For false christs and false prophets will rise and show **great signs and wonders to deceive, if possible, even the elect*** (Matthew 24:24). (Emphasis added.)

"Then I saw another beast coming out of the earth, *and he had two horns like a lamb and spoke like a dragon. And he exercises all the authority of the first beast in his presence, and causes the earth and those who dwell in it to worship the first beast, whose deadly wound was healed.* **He performs great signs**, *so that he even makes fire come down from heaven on the earth in the sight of men.* **And he deceives those who dwell on the earth by those signs which he was granted to do** *in the sight of the beast, telling those who dwell on the earth to make an image to the beast who was wounded by the sword and lived"* (Revelation 13:11–14). (Emphasis added.)

We shouldn't attempt to move in spiritual matters until we've heard from the Lord *first.* We are not to believe every spirit but rather we are to test every spirit as to whether it is of God. (See 1 John 4:1–2 as to *how* we are to carry out these tests.) Our presumptions of facts, timing, tasks, assignments and goals can potentially lead to disaster. (Read carefully the account about the "Seven Sons of Sceva" in Acts 19:13–17). Our Heavenly Father is not seeking independent contractors. He is seeking a relationship with obedient children who will demonstrate their affection and love for Him *by naturally desiring* to carry out His will in all matters. We cannot carry out the Lord's will *unless* we **know** and hear from Him *first.* As we begin to intimately know and love Jesus relationally, then we will begin to be able to discern His voice—a skill that improves with repetition. As we start hearing His voice, *then* we are able to lovingly please Him through our obedient responses.

*"My sheep **hear** My voice, and **I know them**, and they **follow** Me. "**And I give them eternal life**, and they shall never perish,*

neither shall any one snatch them out of My hand (John 10:27–28). (Emphasis added.)

Therefore we make it our aim, whether present or absent, to be well pleasing to Him (2 Corinthians 5:9).

*Now by this we know that we **know** Him, **if** we **keep** His commandments...But whoever **keeps** His word, truly the love of God is perfected in him. By this we know that we are in Him* (1 John 2:3, 5). (Emphasis added.)

As we learn to hear God's voice, we will discover exactly what the Lord Jesus and or Our Father through the Holy Spirit would have us do, or say or think. It becomes a present tense reality. We become more child-like in our dependence on His direction and guidance for every matter.

We can start by asking Him even the simplest questions:

- *Father, what do You want me to do right now?*

- *What do You want me to say in this matter?*

- *To whom do I say this?*

- *Is now a good time, or is it better that I wait?*

- *Where is the next place You want me to go?*

*...for it is God who works in you **both** to will and to do for His good pleasure* (Philippians 2:13). (Emphasis added.)

Then Jesus called a little child to Him, set him in the midst of them, and said, "Assuredly , I say to you, unless you are converted and become as little children, you will by no means enter the kingdom of heaven" (Matthew 18:2–3).

We can overcome the stealth of the enemy if we follow the direction of the Lord by means of His Holy Spirit's gifts of wisdom and discernment (1 Corinthians 12:8,10) and prioritize obedience to God. The ultimate overcomers can be seen in Revelation 12:10–11).

*Then I heard a loud voice saying in heaven, "Now salvation, and strength, and the **kingdom** of our God, and the **power** of His Christ have come, for the accuser of our brethren, who accused them before our God day and night, has been cast down." And they overcame him by the blood of the lamb and by the word of their testimony, and they did not love their lives to the death* (Revelation 12:10–11). (Emphasis added.)

Your kingdom come. Your will be done on earth as it is in heaven (Matthew 6:10).

"Thy will be done" is the essence of His Kingdom. *Without obedience, there is no Kingdom of God.* There is no genuine power of Christ unless it is preceded by Kingdom obedience. **Without obedience, there is no Kingdom of God.** As we obey God *first,* the world is then able to see the genuine power of His Kingdom. Then we, as a result, will partake in His divine power of miracles, deliverances and prophecy. The correct order of God's priorities results in Him being glorified forever.

Notice the priority of the syntax of the words in the verse cited below. First comes the Kingdom of God (obedience) and then the power of Christ flows. As God's power flows, all the credit and glory are ascribed to Him.

For Yours is the kingdom and the power and the glory forever (Matthew 6:13).

Chapter 10

Tiny Little Pieces
Fat Shepherds and Weak, Scattered Sheep

In the introduction of my 2003 book called "God's Got a Problem (On His Hands)", I explained the motivation for the book.

Suffice it to say as a summary, after a decade of early independent rebellion as a young adult, the Lord arranged my circumstances so that I was forced to make a decision regarding who would continue to be the main influence in my life. I, as a previously independent contractor separate from God, had done a wonderful job of creating a mess of my personal life situations.

After dedicating my life to the Lord, my personal growth continued with a Catholic church-sponsored event entitled "Life in the Spirit" seminar. It was there that I received a Pentecostal baptism and was introduced to the gifts of the Holy Spirit.

During that three-day event, one of my mentors handed me a note indicating that several people had been praying for me leading up to the seminar. The verses that I was given referred to the warning in James that not many should become teachers of the Scripture due to being held to a higher standard of accountability. I shuddered. Nevertheless, the proclamation in the note was that I would become a teacher of God's word.

Years later, an opportunity to teach at a Bible college in Mexico for four and a half years along with nearly a decade of jail chaplain ministry proved the accuracy of that prophecy in regards to my personal teaching roles.

This handwritten note also emphasized Ezekiel chapters 33 and 34 in the context of becoming a watchman. My first book dealt with Ezekiel 33 relative to judgment being brought to our country. However, the latter chapters of this current work deal more with Ezekiel 34, which address the sad condition of the Lord's flock, and the responsibility of the flock's shepherds for their weak, sickly condition.

I am certainly not writing this book to win any sort of popularity contest, nor was writing this book my idea—it was the Lord's. I understand the temptation to shoot the messenger; it is easy to do. But I urge leadership to hold their collective fire by first prayerfully and carefully pondering the reformation points proffered. Please engage by "chewing the meat and spitting out the bones" or in other words, "*If* the shoe fits…"

This current chapter is *not* designed to address God lifting His protective hand from us *as a nation*. The removal of His Divine national protection is already underway. The judgment coming to our country has been already been addressed in detail in my 2003 book "God's Got a Problem (on His Hands)" and in other more current works from Rabbi Jonathan Cahn ("The Harbinger") and Pastor Mark Biltz ("The Blood Moons").

Since the publication of my initial book, the degradation of our culture has continued unabated. Our country has continued *to institutionalize* evil into its laws, government operations and educational systems. We have judicially and officially rejected God's framework for the family, the preservation of innocent life and our identity in Him as a Christian nation. To a large degree, *we have collectively jettisoned* God's laws of protection. This trend has been affirmed recently with a declaration from our national head of state that we are no longer a Christian nation.

Are we bragging?

What happens when a previously Christian nation tears up God's blueprint into tiny pieces and throws those pieces back in His face? Has anyone recently read Deuteronomy chapter 28 regarding man's behavior that produces God's blessings versus man's behavior that produces God's curses? A review of that chapter is simultaneously quite sobering and productive. If there is any temptation to dismiss the contents of Deuteronomy chapter 28 due to its alleged irrelevance based on its Old Testament location, I would refer you below to a couple of New Testament verses, which may put it into context:

All Scripture is given by inspiration of God, and is profitable for doctrine, for reproof, for correction, for instruction in righteousness, (2 Timothy 3:16). (Emphasis added.)

Jesus Christ is the same yesterday, today, and forever (Hebrews 13:8). (Emphasis added.)

I am personally convinced that God has heard us loud and clear as a nation. He will not force Himself on anyone. If one desires additional clarification relative to what can be expected when God lifts His protective hand off of a rebellious nation, I would recommend two books by Messianic Rabbi Jonathan Cahn entitled "The Harbinger" and "The Mystery of the Shemitah", as I mentioned in Chapter 9. I would encourage the reader not to delay in reading both of these books.

However, the primary purpose of this chapter is to address how more than a few of the Christian Church's contemporary leaders have *not* been feeding our Father's flock. Whatever motivated this dereliction of duty on the part of our leaders, only the Father knows. Regardless of the cause, the Father's sheep are confused, scattered and starving, and our Father wants it stopped. *Now*!

I understand that the nature of this book can be perceived as confrontational to some leaders. But that is precisely the problem with deception: If you ask a collective group of listeners about who may be currently deceived, you would probably *not* see many hands raised. That is the very nature of deception. Often it's a case of "you don't know what you don't know".

My people are destroyed for lack of knowledge. Because you have rejected knowledge, I also reject you from being priest for Me. *Because you have forgotten the law of your God, I also will forget your children.* ***And it shall be: like people, like priest.*** *So I will punish them for their ways, and reward them for their deeds. For they shall eat, but not have enough; They shall commit harlotry, but not increase****; because they have ceased obeying the Lord*** (Hosea 4:6,9–10). (Emphasis added.)

The luxury of waiting to decide what is truth versus what is deceit is no longer available. The previously unfathomable notion of American Christian persecution is upon us. We're now the ones on the outside looking in. Borrowing a ***paraphrased*** inspiration from Thomas Paine, *these are the times that **will** try mans' souls*. We have finally arrived at the post-Christian era in North America. And if we naïvely believe that we're so special in God's eyes or that we are exempt from suffering for the faith, forget it. The shepherds who taught us that as Gentiles we will not be around for the coming tribulation were wrong.

Dead wrong.

In general, the shepherds have instructed the flock that it will be the Jews "left behind after the rapture", and as such, will be the ones assigned to carry out the end time worldwide Gospel witness while suffering for the faith. Somehow, only we "special" Gentiles deserve "distinguished departure treatment for outbound flights away from the tribulation-filled earth".

This belief is taught in spite of Paul's teaching about what the "one new man in Christ" looks like with *the merger* of the commonwealth of Israel with the foreign Gentile in Ephesians 2. Whatever happened to Paul's teachings that *in Christ there is no Jew or Greek*? Was Paul incorrect? Was God only kidding when He was in the process of forming the "one new man" in Christ in whom there is neither Greek nor Jew?

This Gnostic, Platonic, Greek *linear* deception of overemphasis of Heaven being the goal of Christian redemption along with a more recent teaching of a "pre-tribulation rapture" that removes only Gentile believers from earth to Heaven is a lie. In this teaching we see God's abandonment of the Jews to their fate in the Great Tribulation.

This separation of the body of Christ as to who goes and who stays is a satanic deception designed to divide the body of Christ once again along ethnic, religious and cultural lines. Frankly, the more you think about it, the more you discover how this deception is anti-Semitic in character. Who do you think would possibly be motivated to spread the idea that the Church of Christ is to be divided once again along ethnic and cultural lines? After all, *who* hates the Jews—God's chosen people—the most? And *who* would love to divide the reconciled body of Christ once again through ethnic separation? Who else but Satan himself!

The truth is we Gentile saints won't be flying out of here anytime before the singular second coming of our Messiah. His second coming will take place **simultaneously** with the first resurrection of the saints, culminating in the heavenly invasion of a rebellious earth. There is only **one** Second Coming of Christ. To have an isolated pre-tribulation "rapture of Gentiles", you would have to invent multiple second comings of Jesus.

*"These things I have spoken to you, that in Me you may have peace. **In the world you will have tribulation**; but be of good cheer, I have overcome the world"* (John 16:33). (Emphasis added.)

Yeshua's return to earth will **not** be a secret, anytime coming. His return to the earth will be accompanied by the shout of the Lord, angelic voices and divine trumpets able to be observed and heard by all. Our meeting with King Jesus in the clouds will be a military maneuver, not an escape from earth. It will be a trumpet gathering of the saints to invade and conquer our earth, vanquish Satan's rebellion and finally re-establish our Father's Heavenly Kingdom right here on "terra firma".

*For this we say to you by the word of the Lord, **that we who are alive and remain until the coming of the Lord will by no means precede those who are asleep**. For the Lord Himself will descend from heaven with a **shout**, with the **voice** of an archangel, and with the **trumpet** of God. **And the dead in Christ will rise first**. Then we who are alive and remain shall be caught up together with them in the clouds to meet the Lord in the air. And thus we shall always be with the Lord* (1 Thessalonians 4:15–17). (Emphasis added.)

*Now Enoch, the seventh from Adam, prophesied about these men also, saying, **"Behold, the Lord comes with ten thousands of His saints, to execute judgment on all**, to convict all who are ungodly among them of all their ungodly deeds which they have committed in an ungodly way, and of all the* *harsh things which ungodly sinners have spoken against Him"* (Jude 14–15). (Emphasis added.)

Blow the trumpet *in Zion, and sound an alarm in My holy mountain! Let all the inhabitants of the land tremble; for the day of the Lord is coming for it is at hand...* ***A people come, great and strong, the like of whom has never been;*** *Nor will there ever be any such after them, Even for many successive generations* (Joel 2:1–2). (Emphasis added.)

Blessed and holy is he who has part ***in the first resurrection. Over such the second death has no power,*** *but they* ***shall be priests of God and of Christ, and shall reign with Him*** *a thousand years* (Revelation 20:6). (Emphasis added.)

Behold, He is coming with clouds, ***and every eye will see Him,*** *even they who pierced Him. And all the tribes of the earth will mourn because of Him. Even so, amen* (Revelation 1:7). (Emphasis added.)

Our job will be to overcome, persevere and be faithful unto death until our collective Hebrew and Gentile Messiah (Yeshua) returns to resurrect us, gather us and lead us back to earth.

"And they ***overcame him*** *by the blood of the Lamb and by the word of their testimony* ***and they did not love their lives to death*** (Revelation 12:11). (Emphasis added.)

"I will declare the decree: the Lord has said to Me, ***You are My Son,*** *Today I have begotten You. Ask of Me, and* ***I will give you the nations for Your inheritance, and the ends of the earth for Your possession.*** *You shall break them with a rod of iron; You shall dash them to pieces like a potters vessel"* (Psalm 2:7–9). (Emphasis added.)

"To him who overcomes I will grant to sit with Me on My throne, as I also overcame and sat down with My Father on His throne (Revelation 3:21).

What is generally emphasized more in Scripture, the resurrection of the saints or their ascension? Which event reveals the more perfect divine fulfillment of Biblical prophecy? Observing the presentation of the pre-tribulation rapture theory, which is emphasized more, the ascension of the saints or their resurrection?

Behold, I tell you a mystery: We shall not all sleep, but we shall be changed—in a moment, in the twinkling of an eye, at the last trumpet. **For the trumpet will sound and the dead will be raised incorruptible, and we shall be changed.** *For this corruptible must put on incorruption, and this mortal must put on immortality. So when this corruptible has put on incorruption, and this mortal has put on immortality, then shall be brought to pass the saying that is written: "Death is swallowed up in victory"* (1 Corinthians 15: 51–54). (Emphasis added.)

Have the shepherds ever taught the flock that the word "rapture" does not even appear in the Scripture? Have the shepherds ever taught the flock how the Hebrew gospel became even more Hellenized after the Diaspora of the Jews in 70 A.D.? Have the shepherds ever taught the flock that God the Father selected the Hebrew nation through which to reveal Himself to the world—not Greece or Rome?

Why has the Lord's flock rarely been taught the great differences between the *circular/cyclical* Hebrew and the *linear* Greek values and cultures? Have the shepherds ever taught the flock whether it even makes sense to attempt to interpret a *circular/cyclical, Hebrew* foundation with an overlapping *(Greek) linear* grid?

176

Have the shepherds ever taught the flock that the early Christian church was negatively impacted by the infiltration of Greek Platonism and Gnosticism? Have the shepherds ever explained these were heresies that overemphasized Heaven as the *linear, final, permanent goal* of Christian salvation along with the subtle idea that our earth and created matter was evil?

Have the shepherds ever taught the flock that the *actual goal* of the Christian redemption is the obtaining of eternal life, which is not a destination? Have the shepherds ever taught the flock that *eternal life* is a restoration *back to a relationship with our Heavenly Father* as opposed to a celestial permanent resting place?

*"For God so loved the world that He gave His only begotten Son, that whoever believes in Him **should not perish** but **have everlasting life**"* (John 3:16).

*Fight the good fight of faith, **lay hold on eternal life**, to which you were called and have confessed the good confession in the presence of many witnesses* (1 Timothy 6:12). (Emphasis added.)

Jesus said to him, *"I am the way, the truth, and the **life**. No one comes **to the Father** except through Me* (John 14:6). (Emphasis added.)

*"And this is **eternal life, that they may know You**, the only true God, and Jesus Christ whom You have sent* (John 17:3). (Emphasis added.)

*For Christ also suffered once for sins, the just for the unjust, **that He might bring us to God** being put to death in the flesh but made alive by the Spirit* (1 Peter 3:18). (Emphasis added.)

Have the shepherds ever taught the flock that the way Hebrews perceive the concept of salvation *varies significantly* from the way Greeks view salvation? Or have the shepherds ever taught that our Father is more interested in our Hebrew-like obedient deeds that *prove* the motivation of our hearts rather than in our Greek-like creed (mentally assenting to the veracity of selected Scriptures, qualifying one for immediate "salvation" to Heaven)?

*"You are My friends **if you do** whatever I command you* (John 15:14). (Emphasis added.)

*Circumcision is nothing and uncircumcision is nothing, **but keeping the commandments of God is what matters*** (1Corinthians 7:19). (Emphasis added.)

*Now by this we know that we know Him, **if we keep His commandments**. He who says, "I know Him," and does not keep His Commandments, is a liar, and the truth is not in him* (1 John 2:3–4). (Emphasis added.)

Have the shepherds ever taught the flock *that beyond forgiveness* the main purpose of God's grace is *empowerment to obey the will of God,* crushing the compulsion to remain in sin? Or do the shepherds teach that "grace" serves as a back door legal excuse to continue in our disobedient rebellion because Jesus "did it all"? How low does that set the bar for God's people? How does that powerless, perverted message of grace that solely emphasizes the forgiveness portion of grace destroy the witness testimony of the Church to the world? What does God's word teach us about the constitution of grace?

For the grace of God *that **brings salvation** has appeared to all men, **teaching us** that, denying ungodliness and worldly lusts, **we should live soberly, righteously, and godly in the present***

*age, looking for the blessed hope and glorious appearing of our great God and Savior Jesus Christ, who gave Himself for us, **that He might redeem us from every lawless deed and purify** for Himself **His own special people zealous for good works*** (Titus 2:11–14). (Emphasis added.)

*For if you live according to the flesh you will die; **but if by the Spirit you put to death the deeds of the body,** you will live* (Romans 8:13). (Emphasis added.)

*He who sins is of the devil, for the devil had sinned from the beginning. **For this purpose** the Son of God was manifested, **that He might destroy the works of the devil*** (1 John 3: 8). (Emphasis added.)

Let's be frank here: The origin of the notion that the main purpose of grace is **only** forgiving our past disobedience rather than empowering our future obedience to God's requirements has **Greek, linear roots**. Satan's **perversion** of the purpose of God's gift of grace as consisting solely of forgiveness and unmerited favor encourages a false belief—one that salvation mainly signifies **a change of location**, a **Greek-linear** notion, rather than a change of our character, a **circular Hebrew** concept.

*To grant us that we, **Being delivered** from the hand of our enemies, **Might serve Him** without fear, **in holiness and righteousness** before Him all the days of our life* (Luke 1:74–75). (Emphasis added.)

If we attempt to do God's will in our lives, we are accused by the establishment of the Church of trying to gain our "salvation through works". The truth is Jesus delivers us from the power and control of the enemy in order that we learn **how** to carry out God's will in our lives. Do the shepherds ever teach the flock that Jesus came to save us *from* our sins and not *in* our sins?

*When Jesus had raised Himself up and saw no one but the woman, He said to her, "Woman, where are those accusers of yours? Has no one condemned you?" She said, "No one, Lord." And Jesus said to her, "Neither do I condemn you; **go and sin no more**"* (John 8:10–11). (Emphasis added.)

*If we confess our sins, He is faithful and just to forgive us our sins, **and to cleanse us from all unrighteousness*** (1 John 1:9). (Emphasis added.)

Awake to righteousness, and do not sin; *for some do not have the knowledge of God. I speak this to your shame* (1 Corinthians 15:34). (Emphasis added.)

*Therefore, having these promises, beloved**, let us cleanse ourselves from all filthiness of the flesh and spirit, perfecting holiness** in the fear of God* (2 Corinthians 7:1). (Emphasis added.)

***For this purpose** the Son of God was manifested, **that He might destroy** the works of the devil* (1 John 3:8). (Emphasis added.)

*What shall we say then? Shall we continue in sin that grace may abound? Certainly not! How shall we who died to sin live any longer in it? Knowing this, that our old man was crucified with Him, that the body of sin might be done away with, **that we should no longer be slaves of sin**. Likewise you also, reckon yourselves to be dead indeed to sin, but **alive to God in Christ Jesus our Lord. Therefore do not let sin reign in your mortal body, that you should obey** its lusts* (Romans 6: 1–2, 6, 11-12). (Emphasis added.)

The world cannot observe our imputed righteousness. It can only see our actual righteousness. We are unable to be effective witnesses of Christ when we live, talk and act like the world claiming that we are "not perfect", only forgiven! Should anyone in the Church be shocked to learn that the world sees only our hypocrisy rather than seeing the power of King Jesus to change our lives from the inside out?

*Therefore, having these promises, beloved, **let us cleanse ourselves** from all filthiness of the flesh and spirit, **perfecting holiness in the fear of God*** (2 Corinthians 7:1). (Emphasis added.)

But may the God of all grace, *who called us to His eternal glory by Christ Jesus, after you have suffered awhile, **perfect**, establish, **strengthen**, and settle you* (1 Peter 5:10). (Emphasis added.)

*But let patience have its perfect work, **that you may be perfect and complete**, lacking nothing* (James 1:4). (Emphasis added.)

*But as He who called you is holy, **you also be holy in all your conduct**, because it is written," Be holy for I am holy"* (1 Peter 1:15–16). (Emphasis added.)

*"**You are My witnesses,"** says the Lord, "And My servant whom I have chosen, **That you may know and believe Me**, and understand that I am He. Before Me there was no God formed, nor shall there be after Me. I, even I, am the Lord, and besides Me there is no savior. I have declared and saved, I have proclaimed, and there was no foreign god among you; **Therefore you are my witnesses**," Says the Lord, "**that I am God*** (Isaiah 43: 10–12). (Emphasis added.)

I desire to be an agent of hope for the bride of Christ. I believe there is still hope for us if we will deal honestly and directly with the theological challenges at hand. Therefore, I am attaching excerpts from a sample chapter from my earlier book entitled "God's Got a Problem (On His Hands)" that addresses some of the deeper questions of the most seemingly perplexing contemporary doctrinal challenges facing the Christian Church today. I truly believe that my 2003 publication was inspired by the Holy Spirit and is even more applicable today to ever-pressing doctrinal issues.

Chapter 11

Grace, Faith, and Works: Linked or Mutually Exclusive?
(Excerpt from "God's Got a Problem")

In Ephesians 2: 8–10, Paul laid out the prospect that we are saved by grace through faith in order to walk in good works. Christians cite versus eight and nine while often leaving out any reference to verse ten. Why is that? Are not these concepts linked to each other?

For by grace you have been saved through faith, and that not of yourself; it is the gift of God, not of works, lest anyone should boast. For we are His workmanship, created in Christ Jesus for good works which God prepared beforehand that we should walk in them (Ephesians 2:8–10).

Let's define the words grace, faith and works listed above in the chapter title.

Grace is typically defined as unmerited favor of God toward man. That definition is accurate when you observe the sacrifice that Jesus made on our behalf to assuage the ire of the Father towards us as rebellious sinners. It has also been defined as the presence of God.

The modern church has often limited the scope of grace to mean only forgiveness of sin. The modern church has often perverted the idea of grace to be an alternative to the requirement and the goal of developing obedient behavior to do God's will.

However, grace has many other purposes and definitions other than unmerited favor and forgiveness. As an example, look at the epistle of the apostle Paul to Titus. In the second chapter, verses 11–12, another purpose of grace is seen. It says *"for the grace of God that brings salvation has appeared to all men, teaching us that, denying ungodliness and worldly lusts, we should live soberly, righteously, and godly in the present age..."* Does that not sound like the Christian salvation is the removal of our rebellious natures by means of His grace?

Jump on down to the 14th verse in Titus. It explains that Christ gave Himself for us *that He might redeem us from every lawless deed and purify for Himself His own special people, zealous for good works*. Does that not sound like the Christian salvation is a rescuing of us by means of His grace *from what we are,* i.e. selfish, egotistical, lawless rebels to be a purified people zealous for good works?

Grace is forgiveness of sin but it is *also* instruction and power on how to participate in the process of liberation from the control of Satan over our lives. In other words, grace *enables* us to do the will of God.

Here is a question for the modern church: Is grace ever intended to function as *an alternative* to obeying God in all things? If you answered "yes" to the above, then I would suggest that there is a lack of understanding as to why Christ came to earth, the meaning of salvation and the function of grace. Go back and read the verses in Titus 2:11–12 and 14 slowly. Now answer the following questions:

- Why did Christ give Himself for us?
- What is the purpose of grace?
- Do the verses in Titus contradict the notion that Christ came to only forgive us and to take us to Heaven?

If they do, then maybe our traditional idea of grace and Heaven as being the means and the goal of salvation should be re-examined.

There are other verses that explain the purpose for Christ coming to earth such as verse 5 in I John 3 where it says that Jesus came to take away sins. In verse 8 of the same chapter, it explains that the Son of Man appeared for the purpose of destroying the works of the devil. Sin and the works of the devil are located and found inside of us as rebels. Jesus intends *to cleanse* His future bride and dwelling place (us) of all the works of the devil by means of His grace.

And you know that He was manifested to take away our sins, and in Him there is no sin. He who sins is of the devil, for the devil has sinned from the beginning, for this purpose son of God was manifested, that he might destroy the works of the devil (1 John 3:5,8).

*Husbands, love your wives, just as Christ also loved the church and gave Himself for her, **that He might sanctify and cleanse her** with the washing of water by the word, that He might present her to Himself a glorious church, not having spot or wrinkle or any such thing, that she should be holy and without blemish* (Ephesians 5: 25–27). (Emphasis added.)

Or do you not know that your body is the temple of the Holy Spirit who is in you, whom you have from God, and you are not your own? (1 Corinthians 6:19).

*Therefore, having these promises, beloved, **let us cleanse** ourselves from all filthiness of the flesh and spirit, perfecting holiness in fear of God* (2 Corinthians 7:1). (Emphasis added.)

We Christians often emphasize that the new covenant is superior to the old in that there is forgiveness of sin in the new covenant. But if we were to study the Old Testament, we would see that there was already forgiveness of sin for the Israelites through the animal sacrifice system of the temple.

The Holy Spirit is the component that is "new and improved" in the new covenant compared to the old covenant. He is the battery to the motor. (See John chapter 16.) Only emphasizing the forgiveness of sin and removal to a spiritual place misses the entire point of why Jesus came. Getting our theology right will make a world of difference on how we live and how the world perceives us in the process of living. We may just get back our witness to the world!

We as Christians really have not understood the point of Christ's having come to the earth and having provided us His grace. As the Scriptures listed above mentioned, Christ came to change us by destroying the works of the devil, to purify for Himself a people from every lawless deed, and to cleanse His bride from every spot and wrinkle. Remember, God's problem is rebellion, and the solution to the problem is obedience to His will. Jesus *first* forgives us of our sins *by His grace* and *then* He *provides* us the *power and strength* to overcome our sinful nature *through His grace* and the Holy Spirit. His forgiveness (grace) comprises salvation from the wrath of God. The power (grace) to obey His will is salvation from the claws and domination of Satan.

Didn't the Lord tell us in Matthew 28 in the Great Commission to make disciples of all nations, teaching them to observe all that He commanded? As we actually do the commission, we may just become the lamp unto the world once again! The world would once again see the real power of the Kingdom of God, and the Church would cease to be such a modern–day joke.

Jesus came to save us *from* our sins, *not in* our sins. The idea of salvation is to sin less and less through the power of the Holy Spirit. Romans 8:13 explains that if we are living according to the flesh we must die; but if *by the Spirit* we are putting to death the deeds of the body, we will live. The issue of salvation is always one of life and death, not Heaven and hell. Go back and read John 3:16. Does Jesus speak about Heaven and hell or life and death? Heaven and hell are real places, but they are not the main focus of the reason for salvation.

The goal of salvation is to end the rebellion against God's will both in Heaven and on earth.

Look at the "Lord's Prayer" and read the words slowly:

"Your kingdom *come. Your will be done, on earth* as it is in heaven."

Faith is defined in Hebrews Chapter 11 as the assurance of things hoped for, the conviction of things not seen. The chapter goes on to show many of the examples of the heroes of the faith. Their faith was proven *not* through isolated mental agreement as to theological facts, but rather through their *obedient responses* to the voice and directions of God. They *did* the things that God directed them to do. First, they had a relationship with God of such a quality that enabled them to hear and recognize His voice when He addressed Himself to them. Then, based on their relationship with God, they carried out His will in the particular circumstance at hand. The heroes of faith in the chapter are labeled as such because they believed, they loved, and they obeyed their God. Their obedience, shown in God directed works, reflected the level or quality of their relationship with God.

I looked up the word faith in the thesaurus to see what comparable words would be used to describe it. It mentioned words such as belief, trust, dependence, fidelity, loyalty, and faithfulness. The common link to the words listed above is relationship. A dictionary definition of *faith* is explained as a decision of an individual **entrusting their life** to God's transforming care in response to an experience of God's mercy (grace.) In other words, a relationship of trust, dependence and belief is formed and functioning between God and man. It takes two people to have a relationship. Again, God loved us first to see if we would love Him back by obeying Him.

Faith is not just a mental acknowledgment of some truths about God. Unfortunately, the modern Church has turned the faith experience of salvation into one of an instantaneous guarantee of relocation to Heaven upon death just by reciting some facts about the life of Jesus Christ. Just add water and shake. Once that is done, there is nothing else that really is required of the individual because "Jesus did it all." One just sits and waits to die, be raptured, or be taken to the spiritual Heaven. If one were told that anything might be required of them from the Lord, that would take away from the work of the cross, and would be in essence and attempts to save oneself by means of one's own works. Is it any wonder that the church has lost its witness and light to the world?! We have the wrong goal and the wrong method of attaining the goal!

It bears repeating: *the goal* of the Christian salvation is the changing of us and not a change of location. If we form a superficial relationship with the Lord, not doing His will, not cooperating with the process of change of who and what we are, haven't we missed the point of the purpose of Jesus' coming?

For example, if someone on earth insults me, and I refuse to forgive him, is that a big deal from God's perspective? Haven't

I refused to obey the commandment to forgive my neighbor, as ordered in the "Lords Prayer"? Haven't we been taught that obedience to God is nice but not essential to our salvation? Haven't we been taught that obedience would be considered a religious work, and that I am saved by faith alone as Martin Luther stated by adding the word "alone" to the explanation of Scripture? Isn't it true that the modern Church teaches that after I raise my hand at the Evangelical Crusade and repeat the four steps of salvation, there is nothing else to being saved by faith?

Question: Am I still saved if I continually refuse to obey God's requirement of obedience? Is it not true that the Bible actually teaches in James 3:24 that a man is justified by works *and not faith alone*? Does the Scripture teach that *faith without works* is dead in James 3:26? We need to begin to ask these tough questions and teach the whole counsel of God.

Question: if the unforgiving person described above were to die the next week, still not having forgiven the offender, with bitterness and resentment in his or her heart, what would he or she be like in Heaven? The next step after hurt and anger is a desire for revenge. If the heavenly transported "saved" Christian were to plot an ambush and a day of revenge for the offender when the offender also should finally arrive in Heaven, and the act of vengeance were carried out in Heaven, what would you call Heaven now? Wouldn't it look more like hell or the fallen Earth under the rebellion of Satan?

You see, the place is not the issue. The problem of rebellion is a spiritual problem that began in Heaven and later poisoned the earth.

Changing the location of murderers does not change them. There is not one verse in the Bible that says we will be changed morally or ethically when we physically die. Physical death does not change who we are.

Question: If I never or seldom obey God regarding the defects of my personality and character by just excusing who I am and claiming that is just how I was made, will I still be saved? What was the point of Christ coming to Earth? Most Christians would say that as an unchanged and disobedient servant, I would still be saved because obeying God is really just a "work," and everyone knows we are not judged by our works.

For the Son of Man shall come in the glory of His Father with His angels, and then He will reward each according to his works (Matthew 16:27). (Emphasis added.)

Actually, we will be judged by our works.

It is true that the man who buried his talent in Matthew chapter 25 and did not obey God was not thrown into the lake of fire, but look where he was thrown. It was a place called outer darkness where there is weeping and gnashing of teeth. If one wants to say that technically he was still saved because he was not thrown into the lake of fire, then I have to say that is not a salvation to which I want to attain.

To understand the context of Paul's explanation of grace, faith, and works in his epistles to the Romans, Ephesians, and Galatians, we must appreciate that many of Paul's epistles were addressing the problem of a group of Jews called Judaizers who were following Paul to most of the Greek towns where Paul was spreading the Gospel. The Judaizers were corrupting the good news message of the Gospel as preached by Paul by attempting to saddle the newly converted Gentile believers with the ritual and ceremonial requirements of the Mosaic law in order to be saved. Many of Paul's letters deal with the issues of the meaning of grace, faith, and works, and their role in our salvation. Paul was comparing the free gift of salvation of grace through faith in Christ against the requirements of following the law of Moses with its dietary, ritual, and procedural requirements. Paul was attempting to combat the poisoning of the new Gentile converts by the Judaizers. Few of the Jewish followers of Christ were anticipating that God, through the Pharisee Paul, would reach out to Gentiles who knew little of Jewish custom and religious faith. A conference in Jerusalem (See Acts chapter 15) had to be convened amongst the Jewish followers of Christ as to how to accommodate this huge influx of new Gentile believers and what to require of them as to the requirements under the Law of Moses.

In his epistles, Paul compares the free gift of salvation by grace through faith with the Judaizers' notion of requiring adherence to the rituals of Mosaic Law. *Paul never compared grace to the requirement of obeying God.* If anything, Paul reminded us in Romans chapter 6 that grace is not to be used as an excuse to continue in sin. Maybe so, but the modern Church steadfastly believes that grace does function as a substitute for obeying God as well as the need to follow any requirements of holiness and obedience. Let's be totally honest. If you were to ask most Christians today whether they would be jeopardizing their "salvation to Heaven" by not obeying God, most would respond that they are "saved by grace" and that anything else suggested to be required of them is nothing other than salvation by "works." Their interpretation of Paul's epistles is that Paul was replacing the need to obey God's moral law with the free ticket to Heaven called salvation through the "ticket master" called grace.

The reality is that Paul *never* sought to remove *the need to obey God* and replace it with the legal substitute of grace. One of the *purposes* of grace, as Paul wrote in Titus, *was to empower us* to be able to live *obedient* and holy lives. (See Titus 2:11–14.)

It is true that Christians are not under the Mosaic Law. We are not required to perform animal sacrifices for the forgiveness of sins or to observe the dietary and agricultural requirements as stipulated in the Law of Moses.

However, Paul did *not* intend to say that we don't have to obey God's will in our lives when he wrote that we are saved by grace and not the works of the law. Paul never intended to state that the *moral requirements* of the Law did not have to be obeyed. Paul was concerned about the dietary, ritualistic, and circumcision requirements that were being placed on the new Gentile converts by the Judaizers in every Gentile town where he would preach.

As Christians, we are *always* under law. Paul called it "the law of the Spirit of life in Christ Jesus" in Romans 8:2. This law is an *expansion* of the moral requirements in the Law of Moses. Look at two examples where Jesus explained that if one were so much as to look at a woman with lust, that person commits adultery with her. That was an expansion of the Law of Moses, which only forbade the actual act of adultery.

Jesus *added the requirement* to the rich young ruler that he was to sell all and follow Him. Jesus told him this after the ruler boasted that he had kept the moral requirements of the Mosaic Law.

Question: Did Jesus come to do away with the law or to fulfill it?

"Do not think that I came to destroy the Law or the prophets. I did not come to destroy but to fulfill" (Matthew 5:17). (Emphasis added).

He came to fulfill it.

Question: Where in any of Paul's epistles does it say that grace removes from us the necessity of obeying God in our daily lives? Answer: Nowhere.

Question: Does Paul ever say in his letters that living immorally and in rebellion against God is o.k. because we are saved by "grace?" Answer: No.

If the answer to this question is "no"; then why are we Christians living and acting as if the answer were "yes"?

It is because we do not understand what God means by salvation and how we are to attain it. Again we have the wrong target and the wrong method of obtaining that target. *Salvation is gaining our freedom from the compulsion to continually sin and serve Satan's kingdom.* (See Luke 1: 67–79.)

Question: Are we to elevate the words of Paul over those of Jesus?

Paul, a bondservant of Jesus Christ, called to be an apostle, separated to the gospel of God. For God is my witness, who I serve with my spirit in the Gospel of his son, that without ceasing I make mention of you always in my prayers... (Romans 1:1,9).

Paul states that he is a servant of Jesus Christ. As God is his witness, Paul said he served God in his spirit in the Gospel of His Son. Paul was serving Christ, not the other way around. We are not to elevate the teachings of Paul, a man, over those of Jesus, the Son of God.

Did Jesus say that obeying the will of the Father was a big deal? How many examples in the parables did Jesus talk about the absolute need to obey God in everything?

Hebrews 13:8 talks about Jesus being the same yesterday, today, and forever. If the Lord has not changed, then take a look at Deuteronomy chapter 28 where it speaks of how we are blessed when we obey the Lord and how we are cursed when we do not. Resist the temptation to blow this admonition off by saying that the reference was only to the Jews in the Old Testament. In 1 Corinthians 10:1–11, it cites several Old Testament dealings between God and the Israelites having occurred to serve *as examples* for us in the New Testament. God's requirement for us to obey Him has never changed, nor will it. We ignore His requirements at our peril!

Question: In the Sermon on the Mount, was Jesus preaching salvation by works? (See Matthew chapter 5.)

Question: Do you think Jesus understood the concept of salvation by grace through faith?

Question: Do the requirements of obedience to the Father's will as taught by Christ conflict with the teachings of salvation by grace of Paul?

The above are not just some cute philosophical questions comparable to how many angels can dance on the head of a pin! They are vital, destiny-oriented issues that need to be discussed and analyzed by the modern Church right now. The times in which we live are too crucial to just blindly stick with our religious traditions and to hope it will all come out in the wash. Jesus talked about people who thought they were o.k. and then ended up in places where there is weeping and gnashing of teeth. (See Matthew chapter 25.)

In the parable of the talents, the man who buried his talent did not obey, and he ended up in a place called outer darkness where the weeping and gnashing of teeth listed above were taking place. 5 of the 10 virgins who did not obey regarding the need to maintain their supply of oil were locked out of the wedding feast. Jesus spoke about two sons and only one did the father's will. Note that both had the status of sons, not outcasts. When Jesus was told that His relatives had arrived to see Him, He explained that His relatives were those who did the will of His Father. When Jesus was asked by the rich young ruler as to what must he do to be saved, Jesus listed some of the 10 commandments and then added the zinger requirement of selling all to follow Him. The added commandment drove to the heart of the issue i.e., *would* the rich young ruler *obey* Jesus in all things? Jesus told the woman caught in adultery that He would not condemn her, but He sent her away with the requirement to go and sin no more. She would be saved from death to life first through the grace of forgiveness and then through obeying the will of God.

"He who believes in the Son has everlasting life; and he who does not believe the Son shall not see life, but the wrath of God abides on him" (John 3:36).

"Who will render to each one according to his deeds": eternal life to those who by patient continuance in doing good seek for glory, honor, and immortality; but to those who are self-seeking and do not obey the truth, but obey unrighteousness---indignation and wrath, tribulation and anguish, on every soul of man who does evil, of the Jew first and also of the Greek; for there is no partiality with God (Romans 2:6–11).

And having been perfected, He became the author of eternal salvation to all who obey Him (Hebrews 5:9).

How do works play into all this?

If we study the heroes of the faith in Hebrews chapter 11, we observe that the quality of the protagonists' relationship with God was *proven* in *how* they *responded* to that which was asked of them by God. Their faith was *proven* through their *obedient* actions to the will of God in their particular circumstances. One begins to see the connection between faith and works. *Obedient works* are in essence a *yardstick* to measure the depth and quality of our personal *relationship* that we have with the Lord.

Romans 12:2 tells us that we are to be transformed by the renewing of our mind. With a renewed mind, we then will be able to recognize His leadings. We will recognize His voice. We then can carry out His will for the particular moment. We then carry out that which He has given us to do.

On the other hand, the impact of vain religious works can be observed in the verses of Matthew 7:21–23. Apparently important, religious people were shocked to see that the Lord was not impressed in the least with their religious doings due to the fact that God was not involved in the process. God, in these circumstances, did not ask them to prophesy and cast out demons in His name. They were labeled by Jesus as those who practiced lawlessness, (they did not obey the Lord), and they had to depart from Christ's presence because He never knew them. They practiced vain religious works, which gained them only rejection by Christ.

Will our works reflect whether we obeyed God or simply did religious activities for our own aggrandizement?

There is a tremendous difference between religious works and obedient works. The judgment that took place with the Matthew 7:21–23 crowd dealt with self-deluded "spiritual" people who, in spite of all their seemingly impressive activities, missed the whole point! The Lord is not interested in our inventing ways to save ourselves through empty religious works.

He is interested in being obeyed!

Rebellion against Him is the problem. Obedience to Him is the solution. Empty religious works never address the problem.

Question: Were those in that group still "saved?" If the Christians' goal is to gain eternal life, which according to John 17:3 is knowing the Father and the Son whom He sent, those being commanded to depart from Jesus in Matthew 7:23 apparently missed God's will for their lives. Will they still have eternal life away from the presence of the Lord? Logically, the answer is probably not. Eternal life is the presence of the Lord through knowing Him, as explained in John 17:3. We need to ask these hard questions before the return of Jesus and not later when it will be too late to ask! If we answer yes, they will still go to Heaven, then we have missed the point and the definition of salvation.

The goal is God, not a place.

Question: Can we continually and deliberately disobey the commands of the Lord and still claim to be "saved?"

He who says, "I know Him," and does not keep His Commandments, is a liar, and the truth is not in him (1 John 2:4).

In John 14:21 it states that if we love Him we will keep His commandments. Jesus repeats the same concept again in verse 23. Also look at verse 24!

"He who has My commandments and keeps them, it is he who loves Me. And he who loves Me will be loved by My Father, and I will love him and manifest myself to him." Jesus answered and said to him, "If anyone loves Me, he will keep My word; And My Father will love him, and We will come to him and make Our home with him. "He who does not love Me does not keep My words; and the word which you hear is not Mine but the Father's who sent me (John 14: 21, 23–24).

If we do not keep the words of Jesus, He says that we do not love Him. If we do not love Jesus, then what is our destiny? If we do not love Jesus, can we still claim to have a relationship with Him? Can we still claim to be saved?

For Christians to claim that not doing the will of the Lord has no consequence as to their destiny is absolute folly. If Jesus Himself linked the concept that the proof of the validity of our relationship with him is shown in our obedient works, then for us to ignore that is both dangerous and foolish. If we try to explain it away, then we probably have a place as our goal versus a relationship with God as our goal. ***Make no mistake, we will be judged by our works as they reflect our obedient relationship with the Lord.***

Therefore we make it our aim, whether present or absent, to be well pleasing to Him. ***For we must all appear before the judgment seat of Christ, that each one may receive the things done in the body, according to what he has done, whether good or bad.*** *Knowing, therefore, the terror of the Lord we persuade men...*(2 Corinthians 5:9–11). (Emphasis added.)

As obedient children, not conforming yourselves to the former lusts, as in your ignorance; but as He who called you is holy, you also be holy in all your conduct, because it is written, "Be holy, for I am holy." And if you call on the Father, who without partiality judges according to each one's work, conduct

198

*yourselves throughout the time of your stay here in fear;
knowing that you were not redeemed with corruptible things,
like silver or gold, from your aimless conduct received by
tradition from your fathers* (1 Peter 1:14–18).

*"**I know your works**, your labor, your patience, and that you
cannot bear those who are evil. And you have tested those who
say they are apostles and are not, and have found them liars;
"Remember therefore from where you have fallen; **repent and
do the first works**, or else I will come to you quickly and
remove your lampstand from its place-unless you repent. "**I
know your works**, love, service, faith, and your patience; **and
as for your works** the last are more than the first* (Revelation
2:2, 5, 19). (Emphasis added.)

*"I will kill her children with death, and all the churches shall
know that I am He who searches the minds and hearts. **And I
will give to each one of you according to your works**. "And he
who overcomes, **and keeps My works** until the end, to him I
will give power over the nations* (Revelation 2:23,26).
(Emphasis added.)

*"And to the angel of the church in Sardis write, 'These things
says He who has the seven spirits of God and the seven stars:
"I know your works, that you have a name that you are alive
but you are dead. "Be watchful, and strengthen the things
which remain, that are ready to die, **for I have not found your
works perfect before God*** (Revelation 3:1–2). (Emphasis
added.)

*"**I know your works**. See, I have set before you an open door,
and no one can shut it; for you have a little strength, have kept
My word, and have not denied My name* (Revelation 3:8).
(Emphasis added.)

"I know your works, that you are neither cold nor hot. I could wish you were cold or hot. "So then, because you are lukewarm, and neither cold nor hot, I will vomit you out of my mouth (Revelation 3:15–16). (Emphasis added.)

And I saw the dead, small and great, standing before God, and books were opened. And another book was opened, which is the Book of Life. And the dead were judged according to their works, by the things which were written in the books. The sea gave up the dead who were in it, and Death and Hades delivered up the dead who were in them. And they were judged each according to his works (Revelation 20:12–13). (Emphasis added.)

"He who is unjust, let him be unjust still; he who is filthy, let him be filthy still; he who is righteous, let him be righteous still; he who is holy, let him be holy still. And behold, I am coming quickly, and My reward is with Me, to give to every one according to his work (Revelation 22: 11–12). (Emphasis added.)

1 John 3:8 tells us that the purpose of the coming of the Lord to the earth was to destroy the works of the devil. Rebellion, disobedience, and stubbornness are works of the devil. These works of the devil are part of our character. We were poisoned with them when man fell in the garden. They were passed down to us from our ancestors. These works of the devil are overcome by obedience in the carrying out of God's will in our lives. Thus, if we refuse to obey God's will, are we not still part of the problem of rebellion? Do we still have eternal life even though we are taken away from God's presence and have no relationship with Him? Is the goal of salvation a change of location, or a change in us? Is that goal of salvation a relationship with the Father and Son or going to a place? We need to answer these questions!

2 Corinthians 5:10 says we must all appear before the judgment seat of Christ, that each one may receive the things done in his body according to what he has done, whether good or bad. Galatians 5:19-21 gives a list of rebellious behavior, which ends with the warning that those who practice such behavior shall not inherit, the kingdom of God.

I have a question: To whom were the books of Corinthians and Galatians listed above written, Christians or not-Christians? Look at the greetings in the beginning of the epistles from Paul and he will identify the group to whom he is writing. In these examples, he is writing to the saints, or in other words to followers of Christ better known as Christians. Thus, it becomes clear, that God will judge us based on whether He knows us and we know Him to the point that we recognize His voice and carry out His will in all circumstances.

Obedient works are a measuring rod based on how well we know the Lord and do His will in our daily circumstances. The *quality* of our relationship with the Lord will be evident through our obeying Him or not obeying Him. Didn't the Lord say that if we love Him, we will keep His commandments?

Why are we not able to connect the dots and see the link between obeying God and our eternal destiny?

Look at John 5:28–29. It speaks of a time when all will come forth from the grave. Those who have done good will experience a resurrection of life. Those who have done evil will experience a resurrection of condemnation.

Hebrews 5:9 speaks of how Jesus became the author of eternal salvation to all those who obey Him.

Matthew 16:27 says that the Son of Man shall come in the glory of His Father with His angels; and then He shall reward every man according to his works.

Whether the verb is obey, keep, done well, know you by your deeds, etc., they all refer to works and whether those works were obedient works. The only logical conclusion is that obedient works or the lack thereof will have a tremendous impact on our eternal destiny.

To summarize, grace, as explained by the apostle Paul, was never intended to remove the requirement that we obey the Lord in all things. Grace does ***not*** do away with the law of reaping and sowing as explained by Paul in Galatians 6:7.

Do not be deceived, God is not mocked; for whatever a man sows, that he will also reap (Galatians 6:7).

The ***purpose*** of grace is to cover us with the imputed righteousness of Christ legally and positionally while we submit ourselves to God to learn obedience. We are to submit to the process of being made into His holy image (being changed). As we are changed into His image, Christ's imputed righteousness on us ***transitions*** into ***actual righteousness*** in us, which can be observed by the world. Christ's lamp of light and life in us brings forth the good works, which the world is waiting to see. We are to submit ourselves to the process of coming into union with the Father and the Son while we are in our bodies, while alive here on earth.

It is all so simple yet so profound. If we obey Him we will live. If we disobey Him we will surely die. (See Deuteronomy chapter 28.) Does this sound like the Garden of Eden choice that Adam and Eve had to make?

The purpose of grace was never to excuse our continuing rebellion against God. It was designed to end the rebellion against God. The Lord's grace first forgives us our sin. The Lord's grace then teaches and empowers us to stop our sinning. It teaches us to obey God.

Through our faith (relationship) in the Lord we are saved by being empowered to love and obey Him, which in turn produces the evidence of our relationship, namely obedient works by which we will be judged.

Chapter 12

The Whole Point
Summary and Wrap up

"But you, Daniel, shut up the words, and seal the book until the time of the end; many shall run to and fro, and knowledge shall increase" (Daniel 12:4).

In the Foreword of this book we discussed the report issued by the Christian pollster George Barna approximately 11 years ago. In that report he expressed his serious concern for the health of the Christian church in America, describing a sickly body of believers who were in need of real change on key measures of religious belief and behavior.

More than a decade later, here we are. We the Church still remain in the dark concerning Father God's real Kingdom purpose and plan. We the Church remain unaware as to the overall construct of His **Hebrew circular/ cyclical blueprint** plan for mankind and our earth. We still operate in a Greek, Western **linear** world **without having even consulted** God's Hebraic, Middle Eastern, **circular** blueprint.

God the Father is a builder. He is an Architect. How can we appreciate the God's goal of constructing His dwelling place when we have failed to study and understand His **circular** blueprint?

Lines and circles are not equal. They do not end up the same.

If we are traveling on the roadway without our Father's destination in mind, do we have a problem?

An airplane pilot once informed me that if an aviator is even a mere two degrees off on setting a correct trajectory at takeoff, the error as the plane is lifting off the tarmac is not very noticeable. However, if there is not a mid-course correction while flying the aircraft, the odds of ever locating the target destination and landing safely are exponentially reduced. You see, the small two-degree initial error expands to an ever-increasing divergence between the objective and the widening erroneous trajectory. The initial error takes on a life of its own.

Enter by the narrow gate; for wide is the gate and broad is the way that leads to destruction, and there are many who go in by it. Because narrow is the gate and difficult is the way which leads to life, and there are few who find it (Matthew 7:13).

We have to get this one right. A lot hinges on what we do with this knowledge.

My people are destroyed for lack of knowledge (Hosea 4:6).

Hopefully, what has been proffered in this book will provide God's map, compass and **divine spark** that will remove some of the last obstacles in the way of beginning to appreciate that God selected the Hebrew people, Scriptures and culture through which to reveal His blueprint plan for all His children. Greece and Rome were not in the running.

The story is not all glum. Of late there has been a modicum of progress to bring together God's two disparate people groups of Jew and Gentile under the banner of "one new man in Christ". However, despite a degree of increased appreciation for the mutual bonds and connections forming between Gentiles and Jews, there still remains a significant lag in revelatory breakthrough to understand the Father's heart and strategy moving forward. On the positive side, there has been growth of the Messianic believer movement.

Still lacking, however, is the ultimate appreciation for Paul's teaching of what "one new man" (**both** Jew and Gentile) in Christ looks like. Brad Young suggests we begin with unconditional love of one another as mutual children of our mutual Father and co-heirs with our mutual "Big Brother" Yeshua who happens to be **our mutual** Messiah, Savior, Baptizer, Deliverer, Healer and soon-coming King.

"In the mystery of God, the church and the synagogue are tied one to another...Love is more powerful than theological dogma and must flow from the heart of faith" (Young 30).

How can this Hebraic-based, 5"R" circular message be so simple yet at the same time so deeply cogent and moving? If it is a download from the Holy Spirit, it will endure. Hopefully, we will be enabled to finally take this Hebraic five-word circular/cyclical Gospel message with all its infinite conviction and restoration to every corner of the world. And wouldn't it be just like our Architect Father to reveal the simultaneous simplicity and depth of the Gospel message by removing all the seals of Daniel 12:4 for our complete understanding of His sovereign plan at the end of this age?

Contemplate: Explaining the entire Gospel with *five circular/cyclical words* that bring conviction with penetrating, simple truth—liberating the captives and the oppressed from rebellion. Does this not sound like the Gospel of Luke 4:18-21?

Consider: *Five circular/cyclical words* that serve the purpose of revealing a perfect, Divine blueprint that never changes its original goals of growing in relationship with our Creator. This blueprint also reveals the fulfillment of our divinely ordained destinies to bring eternal life to thirsty and dying people through representing and imparting the Godhead.

Reflect: *Five circular/cyclical words* that describe a rebellious, competitive spiritual force (Genesis 3; Isaiah 14), imposing a pernicious invasion of enslavement to self, pride, lusts and violence.

Ponder: *Five circular/cyclical words* that portray the Father's final solution to man's loss of life and purpose by using Old Testament symbolic, prophetic illustrations of both a fully divine and fully human Jesus the Messiah (Yeshua Ha Mashiach). He would fulfill Hebrew prophecy by coming to earth in human form to destroy the works of the rebel, reconcile man back to the Father and become the appeasement of divine wrath so that we might live in righteousness (1 Peter 2:24, 3:18; 1 John 3:8).

Study: *Five circular/cyclical* words that illustrate the "aliyah" circular nature of our loving Father who yearns for the return of His errant children back to Him. *Five circular words* that reveal the restorative nature of our Father's heart seen in multiple returns and restorations of the Hebrew people back to their God and bequeathed homeland. *Five circular words* that demonstrate the Father's undying love which *also* apply to us Gentiles as we study the parable of the Prodigal Son in the New Testament. *Five circular words* that explain that we Gentile children are also provided that same opportunity to experience God's second chance of forgiveness and liberation from the bondage of sin. The obedience of Yeshua fulfilled the Hebrew prophetical (Isaiah 53) death sacrifice, resulting in man's redemption and reconciliation back *to eternal life* (John 17:3).

Meditate: *Five circular/ cyclical words* reveal that we are children of the Most High God who is the Beginning and the

End (Revelation 22:13), the blueprint and the ceremonial yellow ribbon at the dedication of the **completed dwelling place** where God and man will dwell together at rest forever and ever (John 17:21).

Imagine: *Five circular/cyclical words* reuniting Israel, including the Gentile branches reattached to the trunk of the olive tree of Israel supported by its Hebrew root system. This results in two groups of believers sharing a common heritage that includes all of the Hebrew covenants from Abraham to Noah to David and beyond to the New Covenant promised in Jeremiah and fulfilled in the New Testament book of Hebrews. These two disparate groups become one in Yeshua our Messiah. East meets West under the headship of Christ and changes the world forever.

I took a small liberty in replaying Kipling's "Ballad of East and West". The change is noted with the bold letters:

Oh' East is East and West is West, and never the twain shall meet,

Till earth and sky stand presently at God's Judgment Seat;

But there is neither East nor West, border, nor breed, nor birth,

when they come from the "one new man" birth.

Epilogue

The Blueprint

God selected only one of the two cultures illustrated in the columns below to represent His blueprint plan for mankind and earth.

Hebrew	Greek
· Circular or cyclical time	· Linear time
· Block logic	· Linear reasoned logic
· Historical encounters	· Systematization
· Tribal/family	· Individualism
· Earthly goal	· Ethereal goal
· Moral virtues (the law)	· Intellectual virtues
· Duty, doing, conscience	· Knowing/thinking
· Faith is trust before belief	· Faith is belief
· Deed	· Creed
· Practice	· Theory
· God rules / man stewards	· Man rules creation w/science

After comparing the characteristics of both groups above, can you guess which one God selected for His blueprint?

References

Authority. 2015. In *Merriam-Webster.com*.
Retrieved November 11, 2015, from http://www.merriam-webster.com/dictionary/authority

Barrett, William. 1962. *Irrational Man*. New York: Anchor Book Editions.

Biltz, Mark. 2014. *Blood Moons*. New York: WND Books, Inc.

Boman, Thorleif. 1970. *Hebrew Thought Compared with Greek*. New York: W. W. Norton and Company, Inc.

Cahill, Thomas. 1999. *The Gifts of the Jews. How A Tribe of Desert Nomads Changed the Way Everyone Thinks and Feels*. New York: Anchor Books.

Clampett, Earl A. Jr. 2003. *God's Got a Problem*. Greenwood: Oasis House.

Command. 2015. In *Merriam-Webster.com*.
Retrieved July 10, 2015, from http://www.merriam-webster.com/dictionary/command

Control. 2015. In *Merriam-Webster.com*.
Retrieved July 10, 2015, from http://www.merriam-webster.com/dictionary/control

Heir. 2015. In *Merriam-Webster.com*.
Retrieved July 10, 2015, from http://www.merriam-webster.com/dictionary/heir

Heschel, Abraham Joshua. 1955. *God In Search of Man.* New York: Farrar, Straus and Giroux.

Inheritance. 2015. In *Merriam-Webster.com*.
Retrieved July 10, 2015 from http://www.merriam-webster.com/dictionary/inheritance

Jurisdiction. 2015. In *Merriam-Webster.com*.
Retrieved November 11, 2015, from http://www.merriam-webster.com/dictionary/jurisdiction

Knowles, Brian. *Circa* 2011-2015. *The Hebrew Mind vs. The Western Mind.* Available: HYPERLINK godward.org

Leaf, Dr. Caroline. 2009. *Who Switched Off My Brain?* Dallas: Switch on Your Brain USA LP.

Pervert. 2015. In *Merriam-Webster.com*.
Retrieved November 11, 2015, from http://www.merriam-webster.com/dictionary/pervert

Twist. 2015. In *Merriam-Webster.com*.
Retrieved November 11, 2015, from http://www.merriam-webster.com/dictionary/twist

Wilson, Marvin R. 1989. *Our Father Abraham. Jewish Roots of the Christian Faith.* Grand Rapids: Wm. B. Eerdmans Publishing Company

Young, Brad H. 1997. *Paul The Jewish Theologian.* Grand Rapids: Baker Academic, a division of Baker Publishing Group. Used by permission.

Made in the USA
Lexington, KY
03 December 2019

58103754R00129